TIRED *of all the* BAD NEWS

Bryan Shortall

Dedicated to my family

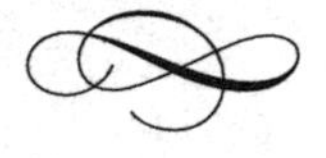

CONTENTS

Acknowledgements

My sincere thanks:

To my family and to Br Adrian and my Capuchin brothers for all their support in putting this book together;
To the people who come to and support the Capuchin friary, Church Street, Dublin 7;
To Br Kevin, Br Sean and all at the Capuchin Day Centre for Homeless People;
To the parishioners of St Michan's Church, Halston Street;
To Paddy Pender for reading over the text prior to printing;
To Patrick, Helene, Ellen and Michael at Columba Press;
To Joe Duffy for his thoughtful foreword.

Bryan Shortall OFM.Cap.
November 2016

Foreword

JOE DUFFY

On Saturday, 29 September 1979, while I was making my way to Galway to read at the papal Mass the next morning, ten-year-old Bryan Shortall was one of a million people who had gathered in Dublin's Phoenix Park for the visit of Pope John Paul II to Ireland.

Outpourings of great joy and fervour erupted spontaneously from the fifteen acres in the park when the Aer Lingus jumbo jet carrying the papal party flew low over the ocean of faithful, but for bright eyed Bryan the sight ignited in him passions which were to endure to this day.

First was his interest in planes. You will learn many things from this enlightening collection of sermons delivered by Bryan, including the call sign for the Shamrock Boeing 747 carrying the Pope – EI-ASJ, named St Patrick.

The second, more profound passion that Bryan discovered that day was his vocation to become a priest – no ifs or buts.

Eight years later he swapped his Dublin suburban bedroom, which he shared with two of his six siblings, for a religious house in the country; Beastie Boys posters were swapped for images of the pope and the General Minister of the Capuchin order.

We can trace the Capuchins in Ireland way back to 1605, since then, with one break, they have gently ministered to the people of Ireland, spiritually and materially. Today the friars are to be found in five continents. In Ireland we know them in their long brown habits, their hooded 'capuche', a simple white cord around the waist and their barefooted feet in modest sandals.

I first came across them through the stories from my Nana Agnes Duffy who lived in a tenement in 89 Church Street, just across from the Capuchin friary and the Father Matthew Hall. In 1913 when numbers 66 and 67 Church Street collapsed into the street, killing seven of my grandmother's neighbours, the Capuchins were there. When the Dublin Fire Brigade had finished their rescue mission in the rubble and ruins the Capuchins stepped in; they were there before the disaster and long after.

Their role ministering during and after the 1916 rebellion is one of the many untold stories that rightly emerged during the centenary commemorations in 2016.

To this day Fr Bryan and his confreres and the many lay volunteers who they embrace are to be seen gently gliding around the centre of Dublin ministering to the homeless, poor and hungry, without fear, favour or judgement.

You will learn many things from this delightful compendium of gentle, profound, thought-provoking, and often witty and whimsical readings.

Bryan confides his love for planes, music, food, people and above all the joy of his priestly ministry.

We learn that U2's 'Where The Streets Have No Name' has a particular resonance for him – it was a hit in September 1987 when he joined the order – but we also learn that the people on the streets, strangers and friends, do have a name, and this is at the core of his vocation.

Yes, of course we all intone from time to time that we are tired of all the bad news but as Bryan's work, and that of the Capuchins, reminds us we still live in a country and community where the bad news of those who fall on hard times is still met by the 'good news' response of others who reach out to help.

It is still one of the joys of life in Ireland that we can still reach out to those in difficulty, and lest we forget this sense of community, neighbourliness', support, dignity and respect that still courses through our land is often powered by members of religious orders, like Bryan Shortall.

You will discover a lot about Bryan's life and motivation, the Capuchins daily life – they are early risers – and his ministry in this insightful and uplifting book.

Bryan reminds us that in the world we live in today, knowledge of water is not simply information googled from your smart phone telling us it is 'two parts hydrogen and one-part oxygen'; in his priestly life, true knowledge of water is thirst.

Joe Duffy
Author and broadcaster
October 2016

Introduction

BRYAN SHORTALL

From time to time I've heard people sigh, 'I'm tired of all the bad news.' Too much negativity plays havoc with our spirit. Exposure to wall-to-wall bad news puts us in bad form and it shows to those around us. Perhaps it was easier in the past to hide from it all because we had to make a conscious decision to turn on the news on the radio or on television. Since the 1980s with 24-hour news channels, hearing of tragedies and disasters, bad news became more difficult to avoid. We all remember where we were when we heard about the dreadful attack on New York on 11 September 2001. I got a text from my brother to turn on Sky News.

Whether it's bad news or good, now our smartphones and tablets light up with breaking news no matter where we are. Today, we can even check our social media mid-Atlantic and send a selfie to our friends at thirty-six thousand feet.

When I joined the Capuchin order in 1987, every Tuesday an elderly friar used to parcel up a copy of the *Irish Independent* and send it to the Irish friars in New Zealand so they could read the news from home. We no longer need to do this as night or day we can interact with our locality from the other side of the world. The astronauts on board the International Space Station, high above the earth, post fantastic photos of our planet as it moves through the day and night.

We need to hear good news. We need that shot of positivity in the arm each day; it's good for us. Being in pastoral ministry today, I am privileged to meet people all the time and I often get to hear their stories. While there are times that I hear about their struggles, there are also times when they are delighted to share their good news, their happy news. As a priest and as a Capuchin friar, I am able to be part of families' big days. I am there to baptise their children. I am at the altar to solemnise their weddings in the church. I have given the girls and boys of the parish schools their first Holy Communion. I am also there with them during the sad times in their lives.

We need to focus on the good news. While I was hospital chaplain, I met some extraordinary professionals who worked above and beyond the call of duty in the service of patient care. When a critical patient comes into the emergency room, no matter who it is, the triage professionals will do the best they can for that person. The patients themselves, despite being in discomfort and pain, and even patients who were given news which meant a new reality for them, often said, 'Father, there's worse off than me.' The level of selflessness I witnessed will remain with me forever. We need to hear this and while we mustn't deny the huge challenges faced it is important to celebrate the achievements too. It's good to hear.

This book contains some homilies I've preached, blogs I've posted, and stories I've heard along the way. In truth, I've written the words with a candle lighting and in prayer. I'm hoping it's good news. In reality, while we can't blind our eyes to the struggles of people, of families, of communities, at home and beyond our shores, it's important to listen for the sounds of good news that emerge too. The news of those people, many of them young people, who roll up their sleeves to help and to support in crises around the world, which helps make the world a better place, must be heard. God does intervene, through the lives of generous and good people, to help relieve suffering.

YOU SENT MY NANNY UP TO HEAVEN

Talk about 'out of the mouths of babes'. I was over with some parishioners who had been recently bereaved and we were to plan the funeral liturgy. Naturally there was sadness in the household as they were coming to terms with their big loss. The house was full with relations and neighbours calling in to sympathise – indeed there was a large group of people gathered inside and outside the house. There were kettles on the boil to make pots of tea and coffee and plates of sandwiches that friends and neighbours brought to cater for the visitors. I am continually amazed by the goodness and generosity of our people to one another in times of sadness. Despite the sorrow, there was also laughter, tears, and stories, as they all shared their own memories with each other. The best therapy in the world is to give time to hear and share each other's pain and struggles at a time of tragedy. This occasion was particularly poignant as the one who died was barely in middle age and the body was laid out in the living room of the family home.

There were some small children there who brought a degree of distraction to the situation and their innocence helped the older ones to cope. One of the young lads, maybe about five years old, looked at me before the prayers and pointed to the coffin and said, 'Is that yours?' In other words, did I own the coffin? I didn't know what to say. What does one say? But another child, again about four or five years old and sporting a pair of glasses, quite like a junior Harry Potter, was running in and out and came over to me and said, 'You sent my Nanny up to heaven.' All the theology in the world couldn't prepare me for what came out of that child's mouth; I was speechless. The only reply I could manage was: 'That's a lovely thing to say, thank you.' And it *was* a lovely thing to say. I have known this particular family and indeed their neighbours for the last few years and I have been with them for baptisms and funerals. One of the grown-ups would have told the child that I offered the funeral Mass for his grandmother and the phrase 'that priest sent your Nanny up to heaven' must have been used. And the little boy remembered.

Priests are honoured to stand at the baptismal font to welcome a new member of our Christian family. In Ireland it is still mostly infant baptisms. We are there to solemnise a marriage between a man and a woman and we stand at the foot of the altar to welcome a coffin and sprinkle it with holy water. These are three big occasions in the life of a family, intimate and emotional occasions, which people will always remember and we are the privileged ones to be allowed inside. To be seen as someone whose prayers and Masses help to bring another close to God or to send someone 'up to heaven' is something I feel will take a lifetime for me to understand. To be *In Persona Christi* as a priest is awesome. Perhaps this child was spot on. And there's no doubt that I was reminded of the responsibilities that go hand in hand with it too.

> Jesus exclaimed, 'I bless you, Father, Lord of heaven and of earth, for hiding these things from the learned and the clever and revealing them to little children' (Mt 11:25).

A DAY IN THE LIFE

I can't help thinking about the Beatles' classic 'A Day in the Life' from the *Sgt. Pepper's* album as I write these few lines. With all the reality shows over the last ten years or so since *Big Brother*, including *The Monastery* where a number of individuals spent some time on retreat in Worth Abbey, people may wonder: what's our day really like as Capuchin friars?

The first thing to get out of the way is the question: 'Are you a priest or a brother?' The easy answer is that we are all called brother; within that some of us are ordained to the priesthood and some are not. All of us have taken perpetual vows of poverty, chastity, and obedience. A way of remembering is this: 'In the order, all fathers are brothers, but not all brothers are fathers.' Hope I didn't confuse you there.

We are a branch of the Franciscan order. The Franciscans were founded by St Francis of Assisi in 1209. In the 1500s in Italy, there was a reform of the Franciscan order and the friars of the reform became known as the Cappuccini or Capuchins. We wear a brown habit with a long hood or capuche with a white cord or rope around the waist. The cord was favoured by St Francis because it is not a belt and therefore simpler and poorer.

Today you can find us on all five continents and we work in a variety of different ministries. Some teach in schools and colleges. Some are chaplains in hospitals, prisons, universities, industries, and to the forces. Some are spiritual directors and counsellors/therapists. Some friars are in the medical profession. Some are in parish ministry or working with those less fortunate. Some friars are travelling preachers engaged in retreat work in schools, colleges, and parishes. We have friars who work overseas in developing countries in justice and peace projects. We have friars engaged in the prayerful support of all in retreat houses. There are Capuchin friars who work in the media and in the spreading of the gospel over the web. And this is just the tip of the iceberg.

The main Franciscan charisms are: fraternity; prayer and contemplation; poverty and minority; ministry and apostolate; and justice, peace and respect for the integrity of creation. Our first charism is fraternity. We live together as brothers and from there go out to our work and ministry. Here in our friary in Dublin city centre the friars spend some of their day on whatever work they are engaged in. One is involved in ministry to the homeless, so he is generally up at 5.00 a.m. to get the centre opened and the kettles and machines turned on. Generally the friars are early risers, but on an odd occasion resting on is allowed!

We gather as a community for Mass at 8.00 a.m. and morning prayer (lauds) at 8.30 a.m. Some have had an earlier breakfast but generally we have breakfast together by 9.00 a.m. Two of us are engaged in parish ministry as parish priest (pastor) and curate so there is a 10.00 a.m. Mass for the people of the parish. We go to various ministries, check mail and email, and we gather again for rosary and midday prayer at 12.40 p.m. Lunch is at 1.00 p.m. As the public office in our friary is open from 9.00 a.m. till 5.00 p.m. we can have visitors and enquiries to the friary office for counselling or confessions. We have the parish office here too so there are parish enquiries and applications for baptismal certificates, and because the parish is old (records from 1700s) sometimes there are people tracing ancestors and family tree lines. We also visit those who are housebound and call to the parish schools.

We gather at 5.45 p.m. for evening prayer (vespers) and supper is at 6.00 p.m. Supper is less formal than the midday meal so whatever is in the fridge is on the menu.

One of the principal ministries from our friary in Church Street is the Capuchin Day Centre for Homeless People. We serve food to up to 250 people for breakfast and 600 for dinner Monday to Saturday. There are takeaway groceries available on Wednesdays all morning and there can be up to 1,900 people queuing for groceries.

Some of the friars gather to look at the *Nine O'Clock News* and chat about their day. We generally retire afterwards, but as with all families there are some night owls in the community too. There is always a visit to the chapel before bedtime to say night prayer privately and the place quietens down for the night.

That is just a flavour of our life and ministry. If you have a look on the web you can find out more: capuchinfranciscans.ie or follow us on Facebook or Twitter. The international Capuchin website is ofmcap.org.

Remember when you went out to dinner for the first time? Or sat at the table with the soup spoon, dessert spoon, dessert fork, starter knife and fork, and the main course knife and fork, the different glasses and so on, and looked and wondered where to begin? And you'd look to someone else for help, and they'd say something like, 'Start from the outside and work in.' Having done weddings, I see the etiquette come into play: the suits, the dresses, the hats, and the speeches. I see the nerves of the best man as the moment approaches when he has to call the guests to order to begin the formalities. We all look to others for guidance when we are somewhere for the first time.

Jesus and the disciples were in Jerusalem and were in the Temple precincts and being from the countryside the disciples were nervous and shy about what to do, and how to conduct themselves there. They sat down opposite the temple treasury and were people-watching. Maybe they were hoping to get some indication about how to walk, or bow, or pray in the Temple. In the precincts of this great House of God built by King David, every step was a prayer and even every breath.

Jesus saw the deference that was being paid to the Scribes 'who like to walk about in long robes, to be greeted obsequiously in the market squares, to take the front seats in synagogues and the places of honour at banquets' (Lk 11:43). He was warning the disciples not to become like them. Beware.

The treasury was a bit like an upside-down trumpet. And it made a noise when money was put into it. These were the days before paper money and so the more money that went in, the bigger the boom it made, and the more attention it attracted. And those in charge, and everyone within earshot, would smile approvingly when someone would make a large donation. What a great feeling to have the adulation of many within the Temple courtyard, and indeed those in authority.

Jesus noticed that a poor widow woman had come along and had made her small donation to the treasury. It barely made a sound as she put it in. No eyebrows were raised here; this woman was invisible. Those in the city were too busy tipping a cap or turning and bowing to some priest with a prayer shawl, for the city was full of holy people. The poor widow just made her offering, and scurried on by. But Jesus saw what she did and he drew the attention of his disciples to her offering: 'I tell you solemnly, this poor widow has put more in than all who have contributed to the treasury' (Lk 21:3). She may have given small money but she gave it such great love. No one saw her and what she did. No one noticed; she was used to that. But Jesus Christ saw her heart and told his disciples that this is the contribution that God the Father wants.

Each of us are called to place an offering into the treasury and like the person who goes away into their private space and prays to their father in secret, God sees all that is done in secret and will reward those who give from their open and generous hearts.

THE VAMPIRE DIARIES

Now and again, to switch off, I look at some documentaries and movies on Netflix and YouTube. Lately I've discovered *The Vampire Diaries* and *The Originals*. Both series are based on a community of modern and cool vampires. It got my attention possibly because for a while as a teenager I was a fan of Hammer Horror and the old black-and-white vampire movies. Later on I read Dublin-born Bram Stoker's book *Dracula* and I've read it three or four times over the years. It's perhaps one of the most famous books ever written.

When I was reading Dracula, the rules were: he cast no reflection in a mirror, he could be repelled by a cross, and he couldn't abide garlic. He never emerged during daylight, and Dracula and all vampires had to sleep in their coffins at night, on earth from their native land. Bram Stoker tells us that the Schooner, *The Demeter,* which Dracula chartered to go to England, carried over fifty earth boxes for that purpose. Now, watching *The Vampire Diaries*, the undead walk in the sunlight if they wear a ring or jewellery fashioned by a witch. They never stop looking at themselves in mirrors, they aren't repelled by crosses, they seem to eat garlic regularly, and a wooden stake may not kill them off.

The human person has a huge desire and need to connect with the supernatural. Along with the vampire programmes and the popular reality TV shows, we see shows where people and camera crews go into well-known haunted houses with psychics. It's as if the spirit world is not that far away at all. In fact the spirit world is very near.

In Easter time, Christians everywhere give thanks for the saving message of Jesus Christ. Jesus Christ came on earth to tell us that God loves us very much and he told us that God is like an Abba, a Father. Jesus spoke in parables to illustrate the closeness of God to His people and how much He loves us. While God is transcendent, God is also immanent, and someone who wants us to be in relationship with Him. One of the most powerful stories Jesus told to show the closeness and the kindness of God was the story of the 'prodigal' son (Lk 15:11–32). He tells this story in the presence of Scribes and Pharisees who are critical of Jesus' mixing with tax collectors and sinners. There is the son who gets greedy and asks for his share of the family inheritance and desires to make his own way in the world. He goes away and makes a mess of his life. When things get desperate, he comes to his senses and decides to ask for forgiveness and returns to the father, who we see has been longing for his son's safe return. This father never gave up on his wayward son. He fully reinstates the son back into the family and throws a party because he has got him back safe and sound. The elder son of the father, despite remaining faithful through it all, is angry and jealous and refuses to share in the father's joy. Even the dutiful son needs some salvation. The point Jesus is making to the Scribes and Pharisees in telling the story is that this 'father' who is prodigal or extravagant in his generosity to sinners is actually God's self-description.

All through his public ministry, Jesus tells the people and his disciples in Spirit-filled words and powerful deeds that it is written that the Christ would suffer. He would be betrayed, arrested, tried, scourged, crucified, and die on the cross. And after three days Jesus would rise from the dead. Witnesses from his group (most of the disciples, his closest collaborators, ran away terrified) came to the tomb where his body had been placed and saw that he was not there. They all had encounters with the risen Jesus who reminded them all that it was 'ordained that the Christ would suffer' (Lk 24:1–53).

Fuelled by the power of the Holy Spirit (Acts 2:1–12), the disciples and their followers were charged with the great mission of spreading the gospel of Jesus Christ (Mt 28:16–20). We are confident therefore that because of these witnesses, and because of their faith and the faith of our parents and their parents before them, we have inherited a belief in God who loves us unconditionally and that through the power of the Holy Spirit we can connect with him anytime through prayer. We also have the prayers of the saints, and those who have gone to the Kingdom of God before us as Jesus promised we would (Jn 14:1–6). We have the prayers of Our Blessed Lady, the Mother of God who goes to her Son, Jesus with our prayers and our needs.

The spirit world, the world of God, is here and now and it is a world of life and joy. And it is through prayer and becoming quiet that we connect with it. God hears all our prayers and is not deaf to our fears and struggles.

THE FIRST FRIDAY VISITS

Working in a city centre parish, one of the nicer things I get to do is to make what we call the 'First Friday' visits. Here we visit elderly and housebound parishioners to bring them the sacraments and to pray together with them. These people have lived in the parish all their lives and they have a wealth of knowledge, experience, and history which they love to share. Listening to them is sometimes like going back in time to a different Dublin and a different church. They have recollections of the joys and sorrows, the hardships and the laughter of their childhood and when they were rearing their families.

Calling to see them, all of them in their late eighties or nineties, I can see they have great inner strength and great faith. They are not theologians in the formal sense, but they have a relationship with God that has stood the test of time. This is the faith that they first heard of at the fireside and in the cradle. And they themselves often tell me of their mothers and grandmothers who taught them how to say their prayers. I appreciate how they easily merge their relationship with God with their own lived lives. It's as if their relationship with Jesus Christ, Our Blessed Lady and the saints seamlessly crosses over into their day-to-day lives with their children, who are now often grandparents themselves. And when the kids call to see nanny or granddad, often they are the great-grandchildren.

The Ireland of the kitchen table has been portrayed in times gone by with the pictures of the Sacred Heart, Pope John XXIII and President John F. Kennedy on the walls. This may be a quaint image that can raise all sorts of lively opinions about where we want to be as a nation into the future. Sophisticated society may say that this is not the real Ireland anymore. When I call to see these people who have given the best years of their lives to the growth of our nation, I see that one of the main ingredients of their endeavours was the old faith. And one still sees a picture of the Sacred Heart or a statue of their favourite saint over the fireplace.

On the first Friday of each month, they are waiting for me to call. RTÉ's Sean O'Rourke or Newstalk's Pat Kenny might be on the radio or Jeremy Kyle might be on the television. We take a moment and turn the sound down. One woman holds her late husband's rosary beads in her hand, her link to the relationship they had which spanned almost sixty years. Another elderly man prays with me as we look across at happy family photographs on the mantelpiece that tell many stories of times gone by. One couple in their eighties have some children's toys around the living room, waiting for the next high-energy visit to nana and granddad.

The reality of age and ill health is never far away and despite some of these people being dependent on medication, and while oftentimes a caregiver is present when I call, there is still a smile on their faces. 'Father, there's worse off than me,' they would say. Whenever I hear of another bad news story locally, or further afield, I think of the many people who are painfully able to look beyond their own troubles and think of another's. This is true Christianity and true humanity and I will never fail to be evangelised by these people of simple, yet sterling faith.

Every time I read this gospel (Lk 21), I turn on RTÉ News or Sky News and see evidence of the prophesies of Jesus to all who listen to him in today's gospel. When we turn the pages of the newspaper or click the mouse for the online news across the world, it seems that the words of Jesus Christ spoken two thousand years ago could apply as much today as then.

> Nation will fight against nation, and kingdom against kingdom. There will be great earthquakes and plagues and famines here and there: there will be fearful sights and great signs from heaven (Lk 21:25–27).

You could be forgiven for just wanting to go back to bed! (Especially when I look out the window and see the wind blowing the summer leaves from the trees on Church Street, and the rain on the dark glass.) This gospel paints a pretty depressing picture already and we're only just into winter.

Jesus Christ reminds us that despite the bad weather forecast or the bad news coming through the media that He is always with us. He is within us to fortify us and help us to speak when we don't know how to or feel the weakness of sin. Look a little deeper and the sun will shine again; He will calm the storms outside and in. He gives generous people all over the world the words and eloquence to halt wars and allow diplomacy to prevail. He inspires so many people, many of them young people, to go to developing countries with the NGOs to help make a difference. He shows the way to our defence forces who are a shining light in the whole area of peacekeeping. At home, locally and nationally, we see such good will to help people all year (but at this time of year especially) in the many charitable organisations.

Jesus is telling his disciples that while the road ahead will be tough, together good will triumph over evil, and to all of us today he calls us to unity and says: 'Do not be afraid.'

JOHN THE BAPTIST

I remember being at World Youth Day in Cologne, Germany, during the summer of 2005. We Capuchins were involved with 'Cafe Cappuccino', a venture where the friars, all in habits, ran a downtown cafe for the week and served coffee, tea and soft drinks, as well as biscuits and cake. It was a pastoral opportunity for people to encounter the friars in a novel way.

A short walk up the street took us to the square in front of the stunning cathedral in Cologne. Thousands of young pilgrims gathered there all day and into the night, praying, singing, telling stories, exchanging emails and adding each other on Facebook. Across the square were two building-sized banners, one saying, 'Thank you John Paul II' (he had died earlier that year). The other read, 'Welcome Benedict XVI.'

Then I heard a loud cry. I looked around but saw no one for a moment, only throngs of people. I looked up a lamppost and there swinging on it was a crazy-looking man with a megaphone, shouting loudly. He was dressed in animal skins and wore long hair and a beard. As I looked and listened, it struck me that it must be street theatre. As the scene went on, I said to myself, this guy reminds me of John the Baptist. And as I stood there with hundreds of others near the banks of the Rhine, I imagined that this must have been what it was like on the banks of the Jordan.

When we encounter John the Baptist in the Bible we find a man full of the Holy Spirit, and we will see this as we draw closer to the liturgies around Christmas time. Even from his mother's womb he praises God in the presence of Jesus Christ. By his words and actions he calls on all of us to prepare the way of the Lord. His preaching is extremely high voltage and it filled people with enthusiasm, and as a result of this many went to him for baptism. Was he the one who was to come? No, he was not the light, only one who speaks for the light. 'Someone is coming after me ...' (Jn 1:27). John the Baptist, through the power of the Holy Spirit, knew the signs of the times and was ready.

It is interesting in our northern hemisphere that the feast of John the Baptist falls around mid-summer and the light slowly begins to fade. 'I must decrease ...' And of course, Christmas falls on 25 December, mid-winter. 'He must increase ...' (Jn 3:30). John the Baptist calls all of us to make the paths straight for the Lord when he comes so that all of humankind will see the saving power of God. The cry of the Baptist rings out in our time as we approach Christmas. We need to prepare the way of the Lord because God is coming to us – to all of us.

THE HOLY FAMILY

There are two different messages between Christmas Day and St Stephen's Day. Christmas Day is predominantly about the birth of Jesus Christ, the Lord of all life. Almighty God came down into the human story as a little baby born in poverty, in a borrowed cave, and laid in a manger because there was no room at the inn.

On 26 December, the Church then celebrates the feast of its first martyr, Stephen. So, the liturgy goes from life to death in a sense. In the Acts of the Apostles, Stephen is one of the disciples filled with the Holy Spirit who will not stop preaching about the good news of Jesus Christ, and those who oppose him want to put an end to him. He is stoned to death as he proclaims Christ and a young man called Saul entirely approves of the killing. Later we meet Saul as he, too, is transformed by Jesus Christ and becomes a champion of the Christian way.

So, in twenty-four hours it is fitting that the Church shows in its liturgy the birth of Jesus Christ and what it means for the world, and how Stephen (and many others – even up to our time) witness to Jesus Christ by the shedding of their blood.

The feast of the Holy Family can be seen as a sign of contradiction, too. In the gospel today we see Jesus getting lost from the caravan of people travelling back to Nazareth from Jerusalem after the Passover. For three days his parents, Mary and Joseph, are beside themselves with worry until they go back to Jerusalem and find him seated in the company of the doctors and experts of the law. Of course it must be hugely traumatic for Mary and Joseph after looking for him. Luke draws out the parallel between how the boy Jesus is missing for three days and later he will, after his death on the cross, be in the tomb for three days.

Let's not get too caught up with the popular images of the Holy Family in that almost clinical and sterile way they can perhaps be portrayed. They had their struggles and fears. Just look at the infancy narratives of Luke's gospel. They must be held up as a model for families today all over the world. Jesus, Mary and Joseph identify with the highs and lows of family life with all its complexities.

Look at the images coming from airports and ferry ports as families are joyfully reunited for Christmas. There's so much joy and excitement around the Christmas dinner table and the living room fireside. Yet, there can be tension and stress too, especially as families make that extra effort. The Holy Family know that struggle. And as surely as our young people come back to the family for Christmas, there are also the looming departure gates. I really pray that very soon our young people especially will be in a position to return home to Ireland if that's what they want. For those that have made a new life and formed relationships overseas, may we always find new ways to make our world a smaller place.

I am also conscious of the families who will have an empty chair at the Christmas table: families broken by emigration, unemployment and death. The Holy Family of Nazareth, the model for all families, knows the struggles and sadness, and Jesus, Mary, and Joseph are with all families as they face the new year with hope or fear.

May this Christmas time and this coming year be blessed for all. Amen.

THERE IS REAL POWER IN MERCY

Some people would say I like the sound of my own voice. I'm well able to talk and I can feel quite at home in any pulpit. Words usually come easily to me. One of my faults is that I don't prepare very well to write a homily.

Therefore, I made a conscious decision to write a Christmas homily for our Masses in the parish and the friary. I wanted to say something about God coming into our human story as a baby in a manger in Bethlehem and how Jesus Christ is the true door of mercy for all. I wanted to tie it all in with the extraordinary Jubilee Year of Mercy in the Church. Pope Francis opened the Holy Door in St Peter's in Rome on 8 December. Here in the Archdiocese of Dublin, Archbishop Martin opened the Jubilee Door of Mercy in the Pro Cathedral.

In Pope Francis' document inaugurating the extraordinary Jubilee Year of Mercy entitled *Misericordiae Vultus*, some lines really jumped out at me, for example, the Pope says: 'Mercy is the force that reawakens us to new life and instils in us the courage to look to the future with hope (par. 10).' He goes on: 'The Church is commissioned to announce the mercy of God, the beating heart of the Gospel (par. 12).'

However, every time I tried to sit down to write something, I got distracted. I was called down to the parlour and the front office to meet different people and I also took a couple of phone calls. At the same time, I was conscious that I needed to go out to buy some gifts for our valued helpers and volunteers in the friary and the parish. I sat in front of the computer screen and tried to put some words together based on some inspiring thoughts from Pope Francis, and the minute I'd begin to get on a roll, the phone would ring.

On reflection, when I went to meet people in the parlour, at the front office, or talked to them on the phone, I became aware that I had an encounter each time with Christ. Someone came for confession and I was able to help them to begin again for Christmas. Some people came for help of some kind or another and they needed me to give them a listening ear and to spend some time with them. One person wanted to help Br Kevin in his work for the many who come to the Capuchin Day Centre for Homeless People. We've been moved by the magnificent generosity of ordinary people.

St Conrad of Parzham (1818–94), a Capuchin, said that when he was called away to the parlour he would respond with 'Yes Lord' as if it was God himself that needed him. Blessed Mother Teresa in her ministry to the poorest of the poor used to say she just saw Jesus himself in a distressing disguise.

Jesus Christ is born once again. We need to open our eyes to recognise him and our hearts to love him, as he loves us very much, and indeed Jesus Christ is the mercy of God. No one is forbidden from approaching the crib; there's a place for you there, and a welcome. Amen.

PADRE PIO'S MITTEN TODAY

Padre Pio is a saint for our time. He has been recorded on tape, filmed, and photographed by many people. I've known and spoken to people who have met him, talked to him, and been to him for confession. I lived with a friar who, as a theology student in Rome, spent the summer months during World War II sitting beside him at a table in the friary of San Giovanni Rotondo. He had enormous appeal and while he was alive people flocked in their droves to meet him, to be blessed by him, and to listen to what he had to say.

Part of his mystique was the supernatural dimension to his everyday life and these examples are well known. Among them was his ability to be in more than one place at once, his power to read souls, his gift of healing, and, of course, the stigmata.

The stigmata – the visible wounds of Christ crucified on his body – caused him great physical pain and, more than that, great emotional pain. It meant that he was an object of curiosity, and ridicule for some. He prayed for the physical marks to leave him but for the pain to remain. Each day friars used to bind the wounds with fresh bandages and cover them with a mitten, a fingerless brown or black glove which he removed for Mass. The visible wounds appeared on his body in 1918 and for fifty years they were a daily source of pain and embarrassment for him. Medical experts were at a loss as to why the wounds continued to bleed over the years. They began to disappear in the months prior to his death in September 1968.

Today, people find great consolation in the mitten of Padre Pio, which is kept in the Capuchin friary. We get a lot of calls enquiring about the mitten or relics of Padre Pio and asking for them to be brought to hospitals or to those sick and in need. While the friars do their best despite their other work to help those who ask for the mitten, we need point out there are important protocols for visiting a patient in hospital. I say this from some years' experience as a hospital chaplain.

Sometimes the only power the sick person has is the desire to be left alone. I remember a patient in hospital saying to me, 'Nice to see you visit me, but even nicer to see you go.' They were simply too ill for visitors. Does the patient or their next of kin know or have they agreed to be blessed by a relic? Is the ward manager or nurse in charge aware that someone from outside is calling to see the patient? Is the visit within the visiting hours of the hospital? Are there other restrictions in the hospital which could prevent visitors, like MRSA or norovirus? It may be that the patient is in an isolation ward or restricted for visiting.

The main source of pastoral outreach in hospitals today is the chaplains. These are appointed by the diocesan bishop/church authority to the hospital authority, are trained and police vetted, and thus lawfully provide for the spiritual and the sacramental needs of the patient. Be aware that there will be further protocols in the care of sick children. It is necessary and courteous for the hospital chaplain on call, day or night, to be asked if it's okay for an outsider to come on to administer pastoral care to a patient, especially with relics of saints.

There is no doubt that the power of prayer can add to the healing and recovery of patients at home or in hospital. Though there are many stories of help through the intercession of saints by praying with their relics, it is the Lord alone who heals. God heals the sick through the great skills of the medical doctors, surgeons, nurses, and other care staff.

When he was alive, Padre Pio spearheaded the building of the Casa Sollievo della Sofferenza (Home for the Relief of Suffering) in San Giovanni Rotondo. Today, it is one of the finest hospitals in south-eastern Italy.

Padre Pio knew the hardships of the sick and also what their families were going through. He would say that while he will always pray for the sick, he would offer every support to the great work of those whose skills are put at the service of patients.

In this gospel Jesus goes to the house of a leading Pharisee for a meal. Pharisees were the holy men of the day. People were intrigued by Jesus and wanted to be around him. They often invited him to their homes and, good or bad, Jesus wanted to meet people no matter who they were. He was known far and wide as someone who performed powerful deeds: who healed the sick, who gave back sight to the blind, who raised the dead, and who told people their sins were forgiven. When He spoke the word of God, they were living words; they set people on fire with enthusiasm.

There were those who didn't like Jesus and his style because he challenged the old order. He didn't rubbish it or say it was to be disrespected. Through the power of the Holy Spirit, He breathed new life into the law. He turned it from a law of fear into a law of love. The great Emmy-award-winning TV presenter Archbishop Fulton Sheen said that Jesus makes the word of God come alive so that if you cut the pages of the Bible, blood will flow, not ink.

Jesus came to serve and not to be served (Lk 14:1). He taught his disciples, his followers, that their ministry was to be a ministry of service. He commanded them – and by extension all of us – that we *love* one another. This love was to be a love that puts the other person first. It is a selfless love. It is like the love of a mother for her child, the love of a dad for his daughter or son. Such love is the key to real happiness and if we try to live by this commandment of Christ it will be a recipe for real contentment.

Jesus saw the pomp and the arrogance among some of the church leaders of the time. In the gospel we are told of the jostling for the best seats at the table, for the places of honour. However, for a follower of Christ, it is necessary to take the lowest place. The Christian message of the lowest place is a counter-witness in a world that glorifies power and control. The Christian idea of moderation tries to talk sense to the worldly popularity of excess and 'more'. The Christian principle of non-violence (which St Francis of Assisi preaches in our time) challenges violence and warfare, of which we see so much today.

While glossy magazines and reality TV attempt to make us jealous of the lifestyles of the rich and famous, scratch a little below the surface and you will find that sometimes all is not well in the lives of the so-called beautiful people. The happiest people are often the people who have little and share it with others with a heart and a half. Of course, there are those who are financially rich and who also give more than their fair share because they believe in the principles of justice. And the more they give, the happier they become.

At our Capuchin Day Centre for Homeless People in Church Street, Br Kevin helps nearly 1,000 people from Monday to Saturday who come for breakfast and dinner. On Wednesdays, over

1,900 food hampers are given to those who call. There is a definite need for help, today more than ever, because many people are struggling. But Kevin would readily admit that the *real* good news story of the Day Centre, which he helped to set up in 1969, is of *ordinary* people who send in donations, who run charitable initiatives, and who volunteer to help make a difference. And many of the volunteers are young people who, with their great sense of justice and fair play, want to help too.

These days our young people are returning to schools and colleges. We pray for you all, especially those going into exam classes. We also acknowledge those who have left school and are at a crossroads, perhaps considering travelling overseas to find work. We pray for you, too. In the words of Blessed Pope John Paul II, 'Do not be afraid.'

We had a wonderful experience recently in Church Street with the 'Rio in Dublin', where 500 young people came to a gathering of prayer and song and 200 stayed overnight to keep the Lord company in an all-night vigil. This was in union with some young people who travelled from Ireland to be with our Holy Father, Pope Francis, for World Youth Day, where two million young people met with him. Jesus Christ counts on all young people to hear his word and to fan that flame, the flame of faith passed on to us by our parents and grandparents – real saints. In this way young people can be at the vanguard of this ministry of service to the church. Pope Francis asked the young people at Rio to be a 'radical force for good'. He also tweets regularly to his millions of followers, in *eight* languages.

Jesus calls on all of his followers to 'roll up their sleeves'. In St Michan's Parish, Halston Street where I'm based, we will have a Mass of remembrance to commemorate the centenary of the collapse of two tenement buildings in which seven people lost their lives on 2 September 1913. Some of their descendants still live in the area and we pay tribute to so many people who lent a hand in a heroic rescue effort. We come from a generous and selfless people who have handed on a rich legacy and the gift of faith in Jesus Christ who encouraged his disciples and all of us to never be afraid to serve. And when we do this we will be truly happy.

MATTHEW THE TAX COLLECTOR

Today is the Feast of St Matthew. He was once Levi, the tax collector who Jesus saw working at the customs house. Zeffirelli brilliantly portrayed the dynamic between Peter and Matthew in his film *Jesus of Nazareth*. Peter held Matthew in contempt for taking his hard-earned money and giving it to the Roman coffers. Things haven't changed that much between then and now because taxes still have to be paid in order for the machinery of the state to keep moving.

All of us dislike when the official envelope comes through the mailbox asking for taxes to be paid or when we see it deducted from the pay cheque. Here in Ireland there is a dislike for the clamper vans and parking attendants who fine cars for being illegally parked or parked over the allotted time. I once parked in south county Dublin near the seaside to go in to buy an ice cream. I pulled the car up onto the pathway and off the road so as not to cause an obstruction. There were about fifteen or twenty cars all parked in the same way. I came back to the car and there was a parking fine on the windscreen. The parking fine attendants were making their way along the row of cars fining all of us. Now, I was parked illegally. I hold my hands up – no arguments there. But that ice cream cost me €80. In fairness, these people are only doing their jobs and they have to pay taxes too.

With the contempt for the tax collector in the gospels, the one who got more than his fair share of criticism was Zacchaeus. He was described as being dishonest in his dealings. He was 'low sized', so that he had to climb the sycamore tree to get a glimpse of Jesus as he passed by. Yet Jesus comes into his life and calls him to a better way. We can see the results of an encounter with Jesus. Matthew too is called to be a disciple and goes on to write a beautiful gospel.

Today, we are called by Jesus as powerfully as He called Matthew. Even though Matthew was seen as a sinner he went on to bring the good news of Jesus to the world. To all who might ask the question, 'Why would Jesus bother with the likes of me?' look at the gospels, read the accounts of Matthew or Zacchaeus. There are people who hardly ever pick up the Bible or the gospels and read the words of life within, but we are called to be the Bible others will read. We are called to reflect Jesus Christ by our example.

ST FRANCIS OF ASSISI

Francis of Assisi – the early years

Francis of Assisi was born in 1182 to Pietro, a wealthy cloth merchant, and to Pica, a lady descended from the nobles of Provence in France. As a young man, he was no different from his many friends, in that he loved to dance, sing and socialise. He loved the limelight and he was dubbed the 'king of feasts' by his friends as he was renowned for throwing the best parties.

Quest for knighthood

He dreamed of becoming a knight. Like the other young men of Assisi, he wanted to excel in the war that was waging between Assisi and the neighbouring town of Perugia. Because he was the son of Pietro di Bernardone, his father dressed him in the best armour money can buy, but he had no skills as a fighter. The young knights of Assisi marched out of the town to war and soon Francis was captured and imprisoned by the enemy for a lengthy period of time. It was while Francis was in prison that he was to realise that God wanted him to do an altogether different kind of fighting. God was asking him to understand that the time was coming for him to serve the real Master.

Encounter with the leper

He escaped and found his way home, where he was quite ill for a long time. His mother and father couldn't understand what had come over him. He was losing interest in his old lifestyle and spending a lot of time alone and visiting some of the old churches in the valley outside Assisi. It was while he was thinking about his future that he one day encountered a leper. Lepers were outcasts in the society of the time as they had a highly contagious and incurable disease. Francis became sick to the pit of his stomach at the sight of the leper and wanted to run fast in the opposite direction. Yet suddenly he was off his horse, and he put some money into the leper's hand. He then took the leper's diseased hand and kissed it. He couldn't believe he had done this but felt so good in himself for having done it.

Francis, go repair my church

It was while he was kneeling in prayer before a cross in the little church of San Damiano that he thought he saw the lips moving and the image of Jesus speaking to him. He heard an inner voice saying, 'Francis, go repair my church, which, as you can see, is falling completely into ruin.' Was he hallucinating? Could this feeling be a mistake. But there was no mistake, he heard the inner voice speak again, 'Francis, go repair my church, which, as you can see, is falling completely into ruin.' In the days that followed, he told his father that he no longer had any interest in knighthood, or following in his footsteps as a businessman. His father was very upset that Francis was going to follow a different path and not the one that he had mapped out for his son. He asked the local bishop, Guido, to speak to Francis and Francis told the bishop that he was no longer calling Pietro di Bernardone his father, but he was now saying 'Our Father in Heaven'.

He began to repair the little church of San Damiano and to beg for money to buy oil to keep a lamp burning there. He also repaired some of the other ruined churches around the area. He dressed himself in a rough tunic with a long hood and tied a rope around his waist, rather than wear a belt, which only the rich wore. He was beginning to see his purpose in life and other young men from the town started to become curious about what he was doing. They could see how happy and free he was and they wanted to join him in his new building programme.

Pope Innocent III

Francis and his new followers lived in San Damiano and they became known as the 'little brothers' or the friars minor. Francis drew up guidelines or a 'rule of life' for the friars to live by and he went to see the pope at the time, Pope Innocent III. At first, the pope thought they were fanatics and he had no time for radicals or fanatics. However, the pope saw something different in Francis and his brothers and realised that this little movement was God's will. He approved their rule of life and sent Francis and his brothers back to Assisi to grow and spread their way of life around Italy and beyond.

Rebuilding the church into the future

As the brothers came to Francis and as the order of lesser brothers grew and spread around Europe, Francis accepted Ciara di Offreducio (St Clare of Assisi) into the order and she and her first followers moved into San Damiano where they became known as the 'Poor Ladies' or the 'Poor Clares', and to this day they live in enclosure and prayer. Francis also accepted lay women and men into the Franciscan family who are known today as the secular Franciscan order. It is clear that at first Francis set out to repair the little ruined churches around Assisi, but as time went on, he found that his work of rebuilding was to repair the church of God, not with bricks and mortar, but with people.

In 1224, two years before his death, he was in prayer on Mount La Verna where he received the stigmata, the bleeding wounds of Jesus, on his hands, feet and side. This is seen as symbolising his commitment to the sufferings of Jesus on the cross. Francis of Assisi died early on 4 October 1226 and he was canonised a saint by Pope Honorius III in 1228. He is the patron saint of Italy and of ecologists.

PREACH THE GOSPEL – IF NECESSARY, USE WORDS

It's not uncommon to see people having a go at institutions on social media. Politics, religion, or taxation – people get exercised about these perennials. Certainly, in Ireland, the institutional church has been the subject of huge criticism over the last few years, much of it the fault of those on the inside. In the lead-up to the Marriage Equality referendum (which was passed by a large majority) there were renewed calls for the total separation of Church and State. Perhaps this is a conversation that needs to happen.

For example, and as a start, I wonder what it might be like to have a conversation in Ireland about what could happen if we take first communion and confirmation out of the schools system. If parents want their children to make first communion they come to the parish and there, along with the support of the parish, there is catechesis and the children are prepared to receive the Body of Christ. One of the benefits of this is it could end the frenetic pressure on parents already hard-pressed to spend money on suits and dresses. The ceremonies (which are very well prepared by great and hard-working teachers by the way) would be downsized and there would be perhaps better attention on the Mass and the preparation of the children in receiving their first eucharist.

Continually we are seeing in Ireland a critique of how power in society – politics, the banks, the church, etc. – was misused over a long period of time. The church in Ireland is getting smaller in size. Small is beautiful. I remain spellbound by St Francis as he knelt before the cross of San Damiano in the little ruined church down in the valley near Assisi. He was confused and afraid and praying for direction and he heard a voice inside, 'Francis, go, repair my Church which, as you can see, is falling completely into ruin.' The message was clear. Initially, he begged for stones and mortar to literally rebuild the broken little church building. But as others came to see what he was doing, they were captivated by his freedom and joy. They too wanted to be part of the solution and not the problem. Still others came along, and this was the beginning of the Franciscan movement. Soon, it would become apparent that the church was not so much to be repaired stone by stone with bricks and mortar, but with living stones, people.

Francis of Assisi was never interested in disobedience or publicly criticising those in authority because he was too conscious of his own sinfulness. He preferred to humbly lead by example. 'Preach the Gospel,' he said, 'if necessary, use words.' He was never interested in self-promotion or cynicism. He wanted to be always a 'lesser brother', a *frate minore*. And that is why to this day in the Franciscan order, we move from place to place and if we're called to serve in positions of responsibility it is only for the time being.

I believe the life of St Francis of Assisi has much to say to today's society. He was happy and joyful because he had nothing. His life was clutter-free so as he could have a direct and unimpeded line to God through Jesus Christ. His life was a prayer. His life is a counter-witness to a society that upholds beauty on the outside, the type which graces the pages of magazines, and where inner moral beauty seldom gets a headline. His life is a counter-witness to those who seek power and control. His life is a counter-witness to the pursuit of fame and the limelight; he preferred to stay in the background and collaborate. His life is a counter-witness to a society that holds that the most important letter in the alphabet is 'I'.

Preach the Gospel – if necessary, use words.

THE PRIEST IS A MAN FOR OTHERS

The priest is a man for others. The priest is not his own. How many times have you felt like that? How many times have you felt pulled and dragged in different directions? How many times have people made extraordinary demands on you? How many times has your day off become an evening off, or a half day? How many times has someone said to you, be careful not to take on too much; be scrupulous about your time off; beware of burn-out? This puts even more pressure on us. Pope Francis named it only last Easter during the Chrism Mass: 'The tiredness of priests! Do you know how often I think about this weariness which all of you experience? I think about it and I pray about it, often, especially when I am tired myself. I pray for you as you labour amid the people of God entrusted to your care, many of you in lonely and dangerous places. Our weariness, dear priests, is like incense which silently rises up to heaven (cf. Ps 141:2; Rev 8:3–4). Our weariness goes straight to the heart of the Father' (cf. Pope Francis Homily, Holy Thursday, 2 April 2015, www.vatican.va).

The priest is a man for others and happiness walks on busy legs. It's good to be busy and while it's important to look after ourselves, ministry to the people of God, the proclamation of the Kingdom of God, is our privileged way of living the gospel as priests. Indeed, to be *In Persona Christi*, not just when we offer Mass, but all the time, is awesome if we actually really reflect upon it. Priesthood ought to be in our blood, in our DNA. We must think supernaturally every day. St John Paul II says in *Redemptoris Missio*, 'This high and exacting service cannot be carried out without a clear and deep-rooted conviction of your identity as priests of Christ' (Pope John Paul II, address to diocesan priests and religious in Mexico, 27 January 1979).

So how do we fuel the fire? I believe we do it by being honest and disciplined people. Honesty comes from the inside and it spills over into all our relationships. These would be relationships with food, with alcohol, with our physical and mental health, relationships with our fellow priests, and with our friendships.

We also fortify ourselves with prayer. Again, as John Paul II puts it, 'Ask for strength from above in the assiduous and trusting conversation of prayer ... Also be faithful to frequent practice of the Sacrament of Reconciliation, to daily meditation, to devotion to the virgin by means of the recitation of the rosary' (J.P. II, Mexico). But a wholesome prayer life as a priest means a lot of things and not merely devotional and religious things alone. And if we are faithful to a wholesome prayer life, it means that everything else will fall into place. I have structures set up in my life that hopefully mean that I will try to live as healthy a life as possible. Since I was a student friar, I have gone for regular spiritual direction. When I began to work in hospital chaplaincy in 2007, a fellow friar suggested pastoral supervision, since hospital chaplaincy would be challenging in so many ways – and it was. And after Beaumont Hospital I've kept it up and I must say, it is just another way I try to remain faithful to best practice.

I was ordained to the priesthood in 1997. I've been in school chaplaincy and then local leadership in two of our friaries in Cork and now in Dublin. I spent three years in Beaumont Hospital on the chaplaincy team there. And now I'm parish priest in St Michan's Parish, Halston St, in Dublin's 'markets area'. I remember getting asked a lot, 'What made you become a priest?' I don't get this question so much now, but I was reflecting on the question of priesthood recently when one of our men was just ordained to the diaconate and he asked me about the ministry of the deacon. For Capuchin friars, all fathers are brothers, but not all brothers are fathers. We are first called to be a brother. Some don't go on for priesthood as they aren't called to be priests. For people outside this is hard to understand; why not go the whole hog? In fact, we're having a general visitation in the order these days. Two friars from our general council in Rome are in Ireland meeting all of us and spending a couple of days in each community. One of the general counsellors is a lay brother, but he's not a priest. The quips from one or two of our older lay brothers are priceless: 'We're going to be interviewed by yer man; the educated lay brother.' So we're not all called to be priests. I know for some their call to priesthood in the order took the scenic route; they were brothers for a few years and felt the call later on. This was not my experience. From day one I was drawn to priesthood in the order; I never saw myself any other way. I have found that being a priest best expresses how I live out my vocation to be a Capuchin friar.

St Francis of Assisi sets the bar very high when he speaks of priesthood. He had an enormous respect for the priesthood. He wasn't a priest himself as he felt genuinely unworthy of it, although we know he was a deacon, as we see him minister as a deacon in the story of the first Christmas crib at Greccio. We also know he was a cleric because he speaks of 'we who are clerics' reciting the office. He accepted diaconate also because he was Minister General of the order.

From the testament of St Francis of Assisi we read:

> Afterward the Lord gave me and still gives me such faith in priests who live according to the manner of the holy Roman Church because of their order, that if they were to persecute me, I would still have recourse to them. And if I possessed as much wisdom as Solomon had and I came upon pitiful priests of this world, I would not preach contrary to their will in the parishes in which they live.
>
> And I desire to fear, love and honour them and all others as my masters. And I do not wish to consider sin in them because I discern the Son of God in them and they are my masters. And I act in this way since I see nothing corporally of the Most High Son of God in this world except His Most holy Body and Blood which they receive and which they alone administer to others. And these most holy mysteries I wish to have honoured above

all things and to be reverenced and to have them reserved in precious places. Wherever I come upon His most holy written words in unbecoming places, I desire to gather them up and I ask that they be collected and placed in a suitable place. And we should honour and respect all theologians and those who minister the most holy divine words as those who minister spirit and life to us.

St Francis was once quoted that if he came upon a priest and an angel he would first salute the priest because the priest consecrates the bread and wine into the body and blood of Christ. This might sound quaint for some but looking a little deeper, Francis of Assisi sets the bar very high for the priest, and sometimes in our lives we encounter solid people who remind us of what we're called to be. Wasn't it St Catherine of Siena who said, 'If you are what you should be, you will set the whole world ablaze.'

From the writings of St Francis again, this time from the 'Letter to the Entire Order', Francis reminds the brothers who are priests of their great vocation:

I beg also in the Lord all you my friar priests, who are or will be or desire to be priests of the Most High, that whenever you may want to celebrate Mass, you do so pure and faultlessly with reverence to the true sacrifice of the Most Holy Body and Blood of Our Lord Jesus Christ, with a holy and clean intention, not for any earthly thing or out of fear of love for any human, as pleasers of men do (cf. Eph 6:6; Col 3:22).

'See your dignity, friar' (cf. 1 Cor 1:26) and be holy, because He himself is Holy (cf. Lv 19:2). And just as beyond all others on account of this ministry the Lord God has honoured you, so even you are to love, revere, and honour Him beyond all others. Great miseries and miserable infirmity, when you hold Him so near and you care for anything else in the whole world. Let the whole of mankind tremble with fear, let the whole world begin to tremble, and let heaven exult, when there is upon the Altar in the hand of the priest 'Christ, the Son of the living God' (Jn 11:27). O admirable height and stupendous esteem! O sublime humility! O humble sublimity, which the Lord of the universe, God and the Son of God, so humbles Himself; that for our salvation hides himself under the little form of bread! See, friars, the humility of God and 'pour out your hearts before Him' (Ps 62:8); humble even yourselves, so that you may be exalted by Him (cf. 1 Pt 5:6; Jm 4:10). Therefore hold back nothing of yourselves for yourselves, so that He may receive you totally, because He gives Himself totally to you.

The call every day to priesthood is our privileged way of ministering. We are called to be *In Persona Christi.* This can be terrifying at times. I think of my sinfulness. I think of my crankiness. I think of my ability to fail, to make a mess of it. I think of my fears. I take too much notice of what others think about me at times. I play it safe. But I'm still here. I've got nowhere else to go. And it's also a great thing we've got. The message of the gospel is exciting and magnetic, especially when I'm around other priests who are enthusiastic. There are some friars and priests who I remember when I feel the burdens. These were and are down-to-earth, good and joyful men. Pope Francis (like St Francis) sees joy as a big part of our call to priesthood:

> For me, there are three significant features of our priestly joy. It is a joy which anoints us (not one which "greases" us, making us unctuous, sumptuous and presumptuous), it is a joy which is imperishable and it is a missionary joy which spreads and attracts, starting backwards – with those farthest away from us.

The call for the priest is ultimately a call to holiness. Even though this is a work in progress, it will take a lifetime. We go forward in joy, humility, and obedience on this way. As Francis of Assisi once said, 'Let us begin again, brothers, for up to now we have done nothing.'

THE FEAST OF THE ASSUMPTION

The Feast of the Assumption of Our Lady into Heaven is celebrated to honour Mary as someone who in a complete and selfless way cooperated in God becoming human in Jesus Christ. I remember Archbishop Fulton Sheen speaking on Our Blessed Lady and he used a lovely image: if we could have pre-existed our mothers and were given a part in her creation, wouldn't we make her the most beautiful, the most special of all women? Jesus pre-existed his mother and he made her immaculate.

And by and large we all have wonderful mothers. Whether our mams are on earth or in heaven, they are still our mothers and we love them. Listen to the requests in the newspapers, on social networking sites, or on radio stations each Mother's Day or at their birthdays and you'll see something like: 'To the best mother in the world ...'

The first reading at today's Mass from the book of the Apocalypse (Rev 11:19; 12:1–6) talks about the battle between good and evil and how the woman (Mary) is a key player in the story of how evil (the dragon) is defeated. Looking at the gospel (Lk 1:39–56) we see Mary in her Magnificat seeking no praise or notoriety for herself on hearing Elizabeth bless her. She is conscious that because of what God has done for her in choosing her to be the mother of the Son of the Most High, she says, 'Holy is his name'. Couple that with the vanity of the dragon in Revelation and we see just how vain evil can be. It seeks to stay hidden in lies yet it wants to be on prime-time television, it loves to grace the pages of the news media, and it wants to be famous. Mary prefers to be like all mothers in putting the needs of the children first, and their own will on the back burner.

We all have our own personal memories of selfless mothers, selfless parents. We pray for all mothers on this Feast of the Assumption of Our Lady into Heaven.

I WAS UNBORN DURING THE MOON LANDINGS

I was unborn during the Moon landings of July 1969. I'm told my mother was encouraged by the doctor to get rest and not to stay up to see the footage of Neil Armstrong and Buzz Aldrin walking on the Moon. I came along in early 1969 and I was born in October of that year. This was at the end of a decade which saw huge change in our country and in the world.

I grew up in the 1970s and 1980s and eventually my mother had six more children. We are all grown up now and my parents are grandparents. I joined the Capuchin order in 1987 and after ten years of study and postgraduate study, I was ordained to the priesthood in June 1997. I am currently assigned to our Capuchin friary in Church Street, Dublin 7, where I am parish priest of Halston Street and Guardian of Church Street.

I am pro life. I believe that the direct killing of an unborn child is always wrong. As a priest this should be obvious, but first, as a human being I am pro-life. My late cousin, Brendan Shortall, was PRO of the Pro-Life Amendment Campaign in 1983. My mother was active in pro-life during that time too. I believe that the unborn child has an equal right to life as the life of its mother.

I believe that zealous pro-life and pro-choice debate which leads to disrespect of the other is unhelpful. I am far more inclined to be impressed with someone who attempts to put across their point in a respectful and reasoned way. Slagging matches lead to more anger and more distrust of the other side.

I believe the unborn child needs a voice. She or he is growing and developing as a unique human being inside the womb. Nature gives the baby the desire to live, grow and thrive. As I write, one of my sisters is expecting a baby, an answer to prayer. The ultrasound scan photos are greeted with great joy and enthusiasm at home when she comes over after a hospital visit. We can even see who this little one looks like. My mother and my other sisters love to feel the baby move and kick and we are looking forward to the baby being born.

The church teaches that all human life is sacred from the moment of conception to the moment of natural death. I hear opinions where the church is told to keep quiet about this, because it's in the news media and in editorials these days. This is perhaps because the church doesn't have a good historical track record regarding child safeguarding. Church leadership stood by while some priests and religious criminally abused children, others were complicit in the cover-up of the abuse to protect the institution. Not only was the church guilty of this crime, but now it has emerged in the UK that some television and radio stars and personalities were sexually abusing children and that institutions – the media for example – knew about this and covered it up, too. All abuse – sexual, physical, mental – is a societal problem. Today the church in Ireland has a most robust child safeguarding policy and it is in place in all dioceses and religious congregations. It is frequently under review and evolving so that best practice can be second to none. It is audited by safeguarding designated personnel in each diocese and congregation and is accountable to the NBSCCCI and the law of the land.

I would argue that the church has a very positive track record in the areas of social justice and being at the vanguard of working with the poor and the marginalised. You only have to look at Christian and Catholic missionaries all over the world in the developing countries highlighting injustices. Closer to home we have church-run homeless centres, social justice action groups, and organisations to assist the needs of the most vulnerable. We can still speak for those most in need and we must.

All of us were once unborn and it was then we needed protection and nurturing. This is a basic human right for the unborn child in the womb. Should not our Irish government, the first to introduce a Cabinet Minister for Children, speak for its most vulnerable citizens who literally have no voice? I pray our elected officials will fight to protect all human life and give equal right to life to the mother and the unborn baby.

The organisers of the fiftieth International Eucharistic Congress held in Dublin included a 'Pilgrim Walk' or 'Camino' as part of the congress activities. Years ago in Dublin there was a tradition of 'doing the seven churches' – simply put, people would visit seven city churches to pray for a special intention. The congress organisers felt that it would be a good idea to resurrect this old practice.

During the week before the congress takes place, and during the week of the congress, pilgrims will be invited to visit the seven designated churches and to pray the congress prayer in each church. Each pilgrim will be issued with a specially designed 'Pilgrim Passport' and each church has its own unique stamp in which to stamp the passports. The pilgrims will receive a certificate on their completion of the pilgrimage.

Each church will be open from 8.00 a.m. to 8.00 p.m., beginning on 2 June and continuing until 17 June, the last day of the congress. Each church will be staffed by volunteer 'Pilgrim Ambassadors' who will give the pilgrims some information about the history of the church they are visiting and stamp their pilgrim passports. This is a little like the practice during the Camino of Santiago de Compostela. The pilgrims don't have to visit all the churches in the one day but can visit them over a number of days. Importantly though, they must finish their pilgrimage with a visit to St Mary's Pro Cathedral, the Dublin Diocesan Cathedral, the last church on the route. There they will get their final stamp and also a certificate of completion. The pilgrimage route is not a long one as Dublin city centre is not very large, and the weather, even in summertime, will be pleasant. Hopefully it doesn't rain!

The seven churches:

St Ann's Church, Dawson Street, Dublin 2

It is part of the Church of Ireland (Anglican Communion) and it is included to recognise our ecumenical relationship with our Church of Ireland sisters and brothers. One of St Ann's many claims to fame is that Bram Stoker, Dubliner and author of *Dracula*, married Florence Balcombe here in December 1878.

The Church of Our Lady of Mount Carmel,
Whitefriar Street, Dublin 2

A Carmelite (O.Carm.) church, it is famous for containing the relics of the martyr St Valentine. Couples from all over the world visit his shrine regularly and especially on 14 February (Valentine's Day).

The Church of St Augustine and St John (OSA),
Thomas Street, Dublin 8
Affectionately known to Dubliners as 'John's Lane Church'. It boasts one of the tallest spires in Dublin. The celebrated stained-glass artist Harry Clarke made some of the windows in John's Lane Church.

The Church of St James, James' Street, Dublin 8
This church is directly connected with the Camino of Santiago. It is also famous as it is located right beside the famous Guinness Storehouse.

The Church of St Mary of the Angels on Church Street (OFM.Cap.)
Completed in 1881, although the Capuchins have been in the area for over 400 years. The church boasts a marble altar carved by James Pearse, the father of Padraig and Willie, two of the famous patriots of 1916. One of the notable ministeries of the Capuchins in Church St is Br Kevin's Day Centre for Homeless People. There is a doctor, nurse, chiropodist, counsellor, and soon a dental service at the centre.

The Church of St Michan on Halston St, Dublin 7
Situated in the famous 'markets area' of north Dublin city centre, it is the oldest Catholic parish in the north city centre – built in 1817. The stained-glass windows were made in the famous Joshua Clarke studios. The pastoral care of the parish has been entrusted to the Capuchin order since 1984.

St Mary's Pro Cathedral, Marlborough Street, Dublin 1
The Mother Church of the Archdiocese and the seat of the Archbishop of Dublin.

These seven churches are among some of the oldest churches in Dublin and have a special place in the hearts of all Dubliners and people beyond.

Following the controversial comments of a popular morning-time radio presenter on an independent Irish national radio station, who used the F-word in relation to the Catholic Church, there has been much comment in the social media. During the next show the same presenter refused to apologise.

It is fair to say that many ordinary Catholics are hurt and disillusioned by the revelations and cover-up in relation to clerical child sexual abuse. It is also fair to say that many Catholics, while they are angry, are prepared to stand up for their church and defend it. A lot of Catholics feel indignant at the pervasive criticism levelled at the church from sections of the media – print and broadcast. One would feel that the media can look down on the church and in their commentary and reportage make Catholics look like some kind of quaint and out-of-date grouping. (There were 1.1 billion Catholics worldwide as of 2005.) They seem to suggest that the cause of most of the social ills in Ireland and in the west is the historical power of the Catholic Church.

There is no denying that in the past the hierarchy of the church wielded huge moral power. Years ago, in rural, small-town and urban Ireland, there was a hierarchy: for example, the local teacher, the local bank manager, the local policeman, and at the top of this the local parish priest. These days are gone now but the fallout continues and we are reminded of this from time to time.

Despite the reportage, and speaking only from my small experience here in Dublin city centre, there are still people contacting parishes for the sacraments. One girl booked an infant baptism for a Sunday in July and there are already some for May and June. I baptised two babies yesterday.

A young couple contacted me on Saturday and asked me to visit their very ill baby son and bless him with the relic of St Padre Pio in a children's hospital. As a result of that visit, two other mothers asked me to bless their little babies in the unit too. I visited two adults in another hospital on Sunday and blessed them. These are only examples of those who feel that they need prayers and blessings along with the expert and dedicated care of the nursing, medical, surgical, and care staff in our hospitals. These are the real miracle workers.

I have had three calls today in relation to people asking to be blessed with the relic of St Pio. On Friday morning last, I celebrated the funeral Mass of a young middle-aged man who quietly came to pray in our friary church all his life, and then I celebrated the wedding of a couple from this parish, rushing from one to the other. I have been invited to Newbridge, Eadestown/Kilteel and Bagenalstown to speak at their novenas over Lent, each to very full churches.

And that's just me, and that's apart from daily Mass and work in the parish office, and working with the two primary schools in the parish in preparation for the first communion ceremony in May. I know many other priests and religious, pastoral workers and chaplains who are very busy in their ministry to ordinary Catholics, Christians and others. We are the privileged ones.

(Incidentally, if you want someone to visit a patient in hospital for a blessing or a prayer, the proper channels are the chaplaincy and pastoral care staff there. Also the patient him or herself needs to consent along with next of kin. All this needs to be cleared by the staff nurse and the nurse managers. And all, of course, within the visiting hours of the hospital.)

No one laughs at God in a hospital
No one laughs at God in a war
No one's laughing at God
When they're starving or freezing or so very poor
No one laughs at God
When the doctor calls after some routine tests
No one's laughing at God
When it's gotten real late
And their kid's not back from the party yet
No one laughs at God
When their airplane start to uncontrollably shake ...

– 'Laughing With', Regina Spektor lyrics

CHANGEOVER DAY

Today, 12 August 2013, is changeover day in the Irish Capuchin province. We had our Provincial Chapter during the first week of July, where we elected a new Provincial Minister, and four Counsellors (I am one of them). We went away during mid-July to pray, and to reflect on what the chapter was asking us to do. A big part of the meeting is spent with one eye on the recommendations of the chapter, and forming communities that will best help the vision to become the reality. As the picture on the jigsaw begins to emerge, the provincial makes phone calls to ask friars to move to new places and to begin new ministries. This is not easy for both parties. We are a small enough province of friars and we all know each other well. It is hard to ask someone to step out of their comfort zone and begin something new and it is also difficult to hear the call, come in and prepare to take a leap of faith.

So today is the day that fifty per cent of the friars are moving to new friaries and appointments. Behind the scenes, a lot of work has been done in preparation. For example, friars who are taking up work in a new place will have documentation from diocesan bishops and the relevant organisations (parishes, chaplaincies and so on). Cars and vans are arriving and leaving with belongings. Gone are the days of, 'Take nothing for your journey, neither staff nor haversack ...' Just the laptop, cell phone, and books. What would St Francis of Assisi say about these *'twenty-first century seraphic logistics'*?

Over the years, I've seen friars pack their bags and move on. It's a humbling experience to witness men say yes to whatever the Lord is asking of them. I am mindful of one friar, Fr Bruno, now gone to God. A former missionary, he moved from Zambia, where he gave the best years of his life, back to Ireland. He didn't have great health in the end but he always said 'yes' to God. I was with him when he died and as he waited for death he was quite honest in saying he looked forward to meeting the Lord. He was even excited about it and he smiled all the way into heaven.

So, by supper time this evening, friars will be settling into their new surrounds. For others, we have been asked to remain for another term. It's what we professed when we took our vows. No matter what four walls are around us, we try to be faithful to living out the gospel call of Jesus Christ, after the manner of St Francis.

THE DRIVING FORCE

I sometimes look back to that September in 1987 when I joined the Capuchins. Like most young people I loved music, and to this day I associate some songs with the time I joined the order. 'Where The Streets Have No Name' by U2 would be one for example. Other artists charting that year would have been MAARS, George Michael, Aretha Franklin, Whitney Houston, Mel and Kim, and even actor Bruce Willis had a hit. I've just done a Google search and I note that in the UK, Rick Astley was No. 1 in the charts with 'Never Gonna Give You Up' in the week I joined the order. Around the same time in the US Michael Jackson had released his single 'I Just Can't Stop Loving You'.

Now, as a forty-five-year-old, it is almost impossible to get into the head of that eighteen-year-old Bryan Shortall. Today, I hear the ads on the radio, 'Dear thirty-year-old me ...' And I wonder what I'd say to that lad if I could go back and talk to him. But he wasn't for talking to. He was full of it, and full of the habit, and full of the sandals, and the friary, and the sense of community, even though he didn't really know what it all meant.

He was scared and emotional the day he joined. He missed his family, and his friends, and his breakdancing, and his deejaying.

He went out with a couple of girls during those last summers. He didn't miss school though, that was one good thing. He hadn't a clue. He was going from sharing a room with his two brothers in suburban Dublin, with posters of the Beastie Boys on the wall, to sharing a religious house in the country with other men, with pictures of the pope and the General Minister of the order on the wall. The question he and the others who joined got asked a lot was, 'Have you settled in?' He used to hate being asked that question. What does 'settled in' feel like? And what's the time-line for settling in? He brought a selection of his LP records and it didn't feel the same playing them in the sitting room of the friary. The older lads didn't wear white socks and they liked Bob Dylan, and Jim Croce, and Neil Young – one of them couldn't even say LL Cool J's name properly. Things were never going to be the same. Not bad though, just different.

Over the years, I went back to the books but it wasn't like school. This time I had a choice in what I learned and I enjoyed this. I began to grow up and learn what it is to be in religious life and I began to learn about the vows I had taken temporarily and would one day take for life. I learned more and more about St Francis of Assisi and his influence on the world of his time and how his powerful message is still relevant in our world today. So relevant that our present pope has taken his name.

Most importantly, I found myself growing in my relationship with Jesus Christ. Not in an over-the-top, Holy-Joe way. There were never apparitions or claps of thunder. I kind of knew that this vocation was from Jesus Christ at the beginning. It is only as I go on that I'm certain it is. I know it deep down – it's the driving force. Like a couple who fall in love, it's a vocation. They work on their relationship; they have their highs, and lows, and their joys and sorrows. For a religious it's a similar dynamic, but perhaps our way of life is little understood in today's world, I would argue.

How does our society make sense of the vocation to religious life today? What makes one thousand women and men religious, including myself, gather with the Archbishop of Dublin at a ceremony to begin the Year of Consecrated Life in Advent 2014? What words are there to explain why I still want to be a religious? I believe it is in me, and I can't walk away. At the beginning and over the years, there weren't any guns put to my head and I wasn't forced to join, and I'm not being forced to stay. As the friars used to say to us, the friary is not a prison. The only reason I'm still here is that I can't leave. I'm trying to find the language to explain it and I struggle. It's like I had no choice and I still have no choice.

And how do we as religious put language on why we still want to be in this religious life? Or quite frankly, how do we make the religious life attractive to people who may be discerning a way of life? I look around at meetings with other religious, especially where there are younger religious, and I don't need to be convinced they believe: I can see it in their eyes, and the eyes are the mirror of the soul. Despite the highs and lows, it is a great thing we have.

RANDOMERS

I overheard two people the other day and one of them described someone who came up asking for directions as 'some randomer'. There's a relatively new word to describe someone as a stranger, or someone we don't know. And while I'm at it, as they say, there are quite a few new words and expressions used more and more today. For example there's 'totes' and 'totes amaze' and 'totes amazeballs'. 'Epic' is another well-worn word. And then there's the word 'whatevs' – whatever that means!

We must therefore all be a 'randomer' to someone. I walk around and people pass me by day in and day out and most of them don't know me from Adam. To the masses I must be just some randomer passing by. Unless you're a rock star or a Hollywood actor or the pope, could you just be some randomer? 'Who was he?' 'Oh I don't know, just some randomer.' It's a cold expression.

I may be some randomer to many out there and vice versa but the randomer has a mother and a father, is a son or a daughter, and perhaps a brother or a sister. She or he is part of a family and perhaps she or he is loved by someone or loves someone. I am conscious that our human love is not perfect but that someone is perhaps loved dearly by another.

I was a hospital chaplain for three years and day in and day out people I never met before came in to the hospital either as admissions for procedures or serious surgery or for an emergency. One could call them randomers, but to someone they are special. The professionalism of the nursing, medical, surgical, and care staff was heroic in the treatment and care of the patients. No matter who came through the doors, especially in critical incidents, there was always a commitment to give the very best care to the patient.

To Jesus Christ we are no 'randomer'. Jesus knows the very hairs on our head. The Holy Father, Pope Francis, in his homily during Mass yesterday said that Jesus is primarily a pastor to us. That means He shepherds us and takes care of us. Today in his homily at Mass for the Feast of the Sacred Heart of Jesus, the pope described God as someone who seeks us out: 'God is always there in front of us ... When we arrive, He's there. When we look for Him, He has already been looking for us ...'

This is the description of a personal God who wants us to be part of his family, who wants to live in our hearts. He is interested in our hopes and dreams and our fears. He loves us, and he loves those we love. And like the lost son and the (prodigal) father, He keeps looking out for us and runs towards us when we begin to return.

'See, I have carved you in the palm of my hand' (Isa 49:16).

Love is always patient and kind. Love is never jealous. Love is not boastful or conceited. Love is never rude and never seeks its own advantage. Love does not take offence or store up grievances. Love does not rejoice at wrong-doing, but finds its joy in the truth. It is always ready to make allowances, to trust, to hope and to endure whatever comes. Love never comes to an end. But if there are prophecies, they *will* be done away with; if tongues, they *will* fall silent; and if knowledge, it *will* be done away with. For we know only imperfectly, and we prophesy imperfectly, but once perfection comes, all imperfect things *will* be done away with.

When I was a child, I used to talk like a child, and see things as a child does, and think like a child, but now that I have become an adult, I have finished with all childish ways. Now we see only reflections in a mirror, mere riddles, but then we shall be seeing face to face. Now I can know only imperfectly; but then I shall know just as fully as I am myself known.

> As it is, these remain: faith, hope and love, the three of them; and the greatest of them is love (1 Cor 13).

When St Paul wrote this letter to the Corinthians he was challenging them to reach for the stars, to be ambitious for the higher gifts. He was offering them a set of guiding principles for their love lives.

This love he speaks of is not the same kind of love that does well on February fourteenth. This is not about candlelit dinners, cuddly toys, Valentine's cards, or boxes of praline chocolates. All these things are good in themselves, but this is not what Paul is writing about. The love he writes to the Corinthians about will not put on any weight and is completely guilt-free if well lived. The kind of love that Paul describes is a recipe for happiness where it matters: on the inside, and this will be radiated to all we encounter.

It is a love that turns away from humiliating the other person, and it does not enjoy other people's sins. It is opposed to scandal and gossip, preferring to tell the truth instead. St Paul's view of love warns us against human prophesying, which is always imperfect. Putting our trust in horoscopes or fortune tellers can be troublesome. Instead, by putting our trust in God, we will always know who can take us forward in kindness.

The love that St Paul describes is also given another name: *caritas*, which means charity. This means charity to all in need, but in its essence it also means a deep love that is selfless, so it sets the bar very high. It is a love for the honours course and it is for the long haul. It is a love that walks the road of life and it is a love that puts the other person first.

Today, couples often choose St Paul's letter to the Corinthians as the second reading at their church wedding ceremony. I believe that the challenge he lays down to the people of Corinth in the first century after Christ is as relevant to us now in the twenty-first. Set your hearts on the higher gifts.

PEACE ON EARTH – JOHN XXIII

Today, 11 April 2013, marks the fiftieth anniversary of the groundbreaking encyclical *Pacem in Terris* (Peace on Earth) by Blessed Pope John XXIII. It was his last encyclical letter, drafted two months before he died. It is unique in that it was the first time a pope wrote not just to all Catholics but to 'All men of good will'. It was written at a time of international tension. The Berlin Wall had been erected in 1961 and because of the Cuban Missile Crisis there were fresh fears of war breaking out on a huge scale.

In the encyclical, the pope examines the situation the world finds itself in in the 1960s. He outlines the importance of order between people in life and in society, between people leading to right relationships and prosperity. He speaks about conscience and roconciliation which gives rise to harmony.

He is critical of the arms race, 'We are deeply distressed to see the enormous stocks of armaments that have been, and continue to be, manufactured in the economically more developed countries' (109). Because of this, 'People are in the grip of constant fear. They are afraid that at any moment the impending storm may break upon them with horrific violence' (111). My mother remembers herself and her friends going to church around that time and praying for peace. Pope John calls for disarmament and calls for nuclear weapons to be banned.

Pope John outlines motives for peace:

> Here, then, we have an objective dictated first of all by reason. There is general agreement – or at least there should be – that relations between States, as between individuals, must be regulated not by armed force, but in accordance with the principles of right reason: the principles, that is, of truth, justice and vigorous and sincere cooperation. Secondly, it is an objective which we maintain is more earnestly to be desired. For who is there who does not feel the craving to be rid of the threat of war and to see peace preserved and made daily more secure? And finally it is an objective which is rich with possibilities for good. Its advantages will be felt everywhere, by individuals, by families, by nations, by the whole human race. The warning of Pope Pius XII still rings in our ears: 'Nothing is lost by peace; everything may be lost by war (60)' (*Pacem*, 114–16).

He mentions the establishment of the United Nations in June 1945 and supports its aims and objectives and its 'farsightedness' in developing its Universal Declaration of Human Rights. He says that education is also integral to the cause of peace as it supports the people listening to each other.

The pope offers a compass in the quest for peace and it is Jesus Christ, the Prince of Peace:

> Let us, then, pray with all fervour for this peace which our divine Redeemer came to bring us. May He banish from the souls of men whatever might endanger peace. May He transform all men into witnesses of truth, justice and brotherly love. May He illumine with His light the minds of rulers, so that, besides caring for the proper material welfare of their peoples, they may also guarantee them the fairest gift of peace.
>
> Finally, may Christ inflame the desires of all men to break through the barriers which divide them, to strengthen the bonds of mutual love, to learn to understand one another and to pardon those who have done them wrong. Through His power and inspiration may all peoples welcome each other to their hearts as brothers, and may the peace they long for ever flower and ever reign among them (*Pacem*, 171).

CHRIST THE KING

The message of Jesus Christ turns the message of our world upside-down. Jesus teaches that it is better to give our extra coat to the one who has none. Jesus' message of the lowest place is a counter-witness in a world that glorifies power and control. Jesus calls for us to turn the other cheek. This challenges violence and warfare, of which we see so much of today. Jesus encourages us to see the beauty of the person on the inside when our world would prefer to highlight outward beauty and strength. Was it Archbishop Fulton Sheen who once said, 'Virtue preserves youthfulness better than all the pomades of Elizabeth Arden'?

The disciples found it hard to understand why Jesus kept preaching that the Christ would have to suffer grievously and die. The established church and its leaders at the time were horrified that Jesus would call God, the One whose name couldn't be mentioned, Abba (Father), therefore equating himself to God. The Romans, who didn't believe in God, were the only ones to actually call him 'King' – albeit in mockery.

And now we see Jesus dying in agony on the cross and while they shouted at him to come down as a price for their belief, he stayed up there because he loves the Father, and loves us all.

And one of the most consoling scenes in the gospel takes place between one of the criminals and Jesus. We can only imagine what this criminal must have done to merit Roman crucifixion. As children in school I remember we called him 'the good thief'. A thief, he was not. Romans didn't crucify people for stealing bread. Romans used crucifixion as a horrifying, agonising act of public disgrace. The criminal who was crucified was to be seen as a non-person. He defends Jesus who is being mocked by all and now by one of his 'fellow criminals': 'Jesus, remember me when you come into your Kingdom' (Lk 23:39–43). While Jesus is dying to save the whole world, he is paying attention to this poor man's confession. He doesn't act as judge and jury, as some of us remember confessions in the past. He asks no questions. He promises, 'This day, you will be with me in paradise.' He doesn't just forgive him, he canonises him.

At the closing of the Year of Faith, we give thanks to God for the faith passed on to us by our parents, our grandparents, teachers, priests and religious, those who support and at times challenge us along the way. We pray for the Holy Father, Pope Francis, and the bishops as we go forward and reaffirm our faith as best we can, with the help of Mary our Mother, our belief in her Son, Jesus Christ, the Universal King.

TEN MONKS EAT ME OUT OF HOUSE AND HOME

The local farmer who took care of the old Penal graveyard in Tisaran, Co. Offaly told us a little of the history of the place. He showed us some of the work he had done cutting the grass, and the ivy from the stone walls. He then said, 'Ten monks are supposed to be coming down here for a Mass tonight.' He went on to smile, 'Ye wouldn't happen to be three of them?'

We were in Tisaran, in the parish of Ferbane, Co. Offaly, to be part of the Jubilee celebrations of the local church there dedicated to Saints Patrick and Saran. St Saran was a local saint who ministered in that area fifteen hundred years ago. The monastic site of Clonmacnoise is further east, on the banks of the river Shannon, the next parish in fact.

Another reason we were there was because one of the first Irish Capuchin Franciscans, Fr Stephen Daly is buried in that small rural cemetery of Tisaran. He died at the age of forty-five in the year 1620, having returned to the little parish five years before.

Stephen was born in the 1570s and left the area to join the newly formed Capuchin reform of the Franciscan order in Europe. He was ordained to the priesthood and ministered in

Belgium. He felt called to return to Ireland and landed back in Dublin in 1615. He then made his way to Offaly to his home parish in the diocese of Ardagh and Clonmacnoise.

Life for Catholics in rural Ireland was very different from those living on the Continent and in Catholic Belgium when Fr Stephen began his ministry. The Penal Laws were beginning to come into force and some few years later they would be at their strongest. Many Catholics were forced to embrace the Protestant reform or starve. Priests and religious were hunted and spied upon and for generations people who wanted to practise their faith had to do so underground. It was on ancient Irish 'Mass rocks' that a priest offered the Holy Sacrifice, with some of the poor congregation keeping a lookout for soldiers. The friars were used to living in community and poverty in Europe and there they were very visible in their Capuchin habits and long beards. In Ireland this was forbidden and the first four friars in Ireland had to dress in secular clothes. They also lived their religious life apart from each other and in fear of capture and worse. The friars were bolstered by new arrivals from Europe in the later years but with the Penal Laws it was almost impossible to minister. Hardship, illness, and even martyrdom awaited a zealous Catholic.

One famous Irish success story, however, in the years before the Great Famine of the 1840s was Kilkenny Capuchin Fr Theobald Mathew, the Apostle of Temperance. He succeeded in calling people to take the pledge against alcohol, and at a time when the country was brought to its knees by famine and emigration;

so many people addicted to drink were supported in the virtue of temperance. The Capuchin order subsequently died out in Ireland, and it was only when a mission left Belgium in the 1870s that the present-day Capuchin Province was reformed in 1885. We friars travelled to be part of the Jubilee celebrations of Tisaran parish and to pay fraternal tribute to Fr Stephen, our Capuchin brother, among his own fellow county-women and -men. We were warmly welcomed by the local clergy, Fr Frankie Murray and Fr Tom Cox. Fr Frankie had a fantastic supper laid on for us, and where he was expecting ten monks fourteen turned up and ate him 'out of house and home'! In the spirit of the rule of St Francis, 'The Friars shall eat what is set before them.' And we certainly did!

When we travelled out the road to the old graveyard, seats were set up and an altar, candles and flowers prepared. We offered Mass with many of the local people who made us feel so welcome. At Mass, led by our Capuchin Provincial Minister, Fr Des McNaboe, with a homily powerfully preached by Capuchin historian Fr Paul Murphy, we paid tribute to St Saran and the other saints of the locality: Sts Mel and Ciaran. We also recalled the faith handed on to us by those mighty women and men who selflessly passed it on at the cradle and by the fireside here in Ireland and all over the world. We prayed with our Capuchin brother, Stephen Daly, who we look up to as a trailblazer for the faith in his time.

At a time when the Irish church is suffering once again – this time for reasons other than Penal Laws – acknowledging the criminal sexual abuse of children by priests and religious, and the cover-up and denial of this by many in leadership, we draw strength from people like Fr Stephen Daly. We also draw strength from selfless and holy religious, priests, fellow women and men, our parents, and others gone before us who inspire us to this day and who urge us on.

THE SCANDAL OF THE CROSS

All Jesus' disciples deserted him on Good Friday except John. Those who followed him and supported what he was doing in his public ministry must have been shell-shocked, terrified, and bewildered at seeing him suffer and die on the cross (Jn 18ff.). Humanly speaking, it made no sense for Jesus to go when the momentum was gathering pace. More and more were hearing him speak words of life to those broken down in sin. People were coming to touch the hem of his garment so as to be healed. Jesus himself was always willing to heal the sick, to raise the dead, and to forgive the sinner. So why this roller coaster of a week, where at the beginning people were crying 'Hosannah', and by the end of it they were shouting 'Crucify him'?

Jesus came on earth on the Father's terms. He always did what pleased the Father (Jn 8:29). He said. 'It was written that the Christ should suffer' (Lk 24:44–48). This was the master plan of God the Father: that He would prove once and for all that He loves His people.

'Though He was in the form of God, Jesus did not count equality with God, but emptied Himself to assume the condition of a slave. And being found in human form he was humbler yet, even to accepting death, death on a cross. But God raised Him on High, and gave Him the name that is above other names' (Phil 2:6–11).

The cross at first glance is a symbol of failure and of scandal. But looking deeper, the cross is the theatre of redemption. For it is here that we are saved from our sins. Jesus never came down off the cross (Mt 27:40). We are loved unconditionally. The cross of Christ is the touchstone for us with the Kingdom of Heaven and it burns away our sins and failures. The good news is the cross of Christ is the symbol of hope for the hopeless. And it is a hope that will sustain us for our journey of life here on earth, and it sanctifies us for our life with God in heaven. There is no need to be afraid.

NOT SOMETHING I TALK ABOUT EVERY DAY

I was in the Carmelite Church in Clarendon Street yesterday to go to confession. The sacrament of reconciliation or confession is not something you hear about every day, but I like to try and go regularly. When we confess our sins, we confess to Jesus Christ. The priest is there *In Persona Christi* and Christ told the disciples to forgive sins (Mt 18:22; Jn 20:21–23).

In popular culture today, it seems that people are more inclined to confess on prime-time TV or radio than through confession. People say to me, 'Sure no one goes to confession any more' and, 'Nothing is a sin any longer.'

As a priest hearing confessions from time to time, I know there are those who are fearful of confession. Perhaps it was because of a bad experience in confession in the past. Sadly, there were priests who got angry and acted as judge and jury and they were wrong to do so. This should not be the case today. Confession today should be life-giving and an opportunity for real renewal. And while I know people may still feel worried about what to say, the priest will always be there to help.

Well, the good news is that people do go. I joined a large queue of people of all ages for confession yesterday. I must have waited for half an hour as people went in and came out of the Reconciliation Room there. And people were joining the queue after I left. The Carmelites (both OCD Carmelites and O.Carm.) in Dublin city centre offer this service each day in their churches and the people come along.

Most parishes have reconciliation services coming up to Holy Week and this too is a great opportunity to make a fresh start. One of the best parables in the gospels is the story of the merciful and generous father, and the prodigal son (Luke 15:11–32):

> Then he said, 'There was a man who had two sons. The younger one said to his father, "Father, let me have the share of the estate that will come to me." So the father divided the property between them. A few days later, the younger son got together everything he had and left for a distant country where he squandered his money on a life of debauchery.
>
> 'When he had spent it all, that country experienced a severe famine, and now he began to feel the pinch; so he hired himself out to one of the local inhabitants who put him on his farm to feed the pigs. And he would willingly have filled himself with the husks the pigs were eating but no one would let him have them. Then he came to his senses and said, "How many of my father's hired men have all the food they want and more, and here am I dying of hunger! I will leave this place and go to my father and say: 'Father, I have sinned against heaven and against

you; no longer deserve to be called your son; treat me as one of your hired men.'" So he left the place and went back to his father.

'While he was still a long way off, his father saw him and was moved with pity. He ran to the boy, clasped him in his arms and kissed him. Then his son said, "Father, I have sinned against heaven and against you. I no longer deserve to be called your son." But the father said to his servants, "Quick! Bring out the best robe and put it on him; put a ring on his finger and sandals on his feet. Bring the calf we have been fattening, and kill it; we will celebrate by having a feast, because this son of mine was dead and has come back to life; he was lost and is found." And they began to celebrate.

'Now the elder son was out in the fields, and on his way back, as he drew near the house, he could hear music and dancing. Calling one of the servants he asked what it was all about. The servant told him, "Your brother has come, and your father has killed the calf we had been fattening because he has got him back safe and sound." He was angry then and refused to go in, and his father came out and began to urge him to come in; but he retorted to his father, "All these years I have slaved for you and never once disobeyed any orders of yours, yet you never offered me so much as a kid for me to celebrate with my friends. But, for this son of yours, when he comes back after swallowing up your property – he and his loose women – you kill the calf we had been fattening."

'The father said, "My son, you are with me always and all I have is yours. But it was only right we should celebrate and rejoice, because your brother here was dead and has come to life; he was lost and is found."'

I've just been to our two primary schools in the parish to distribute blessed ashes. The students excitedly queued for a blessing and were delighted to sport their ashes to each other. Some came back for more. Wearing the blessed ashes is a visible reminder that I am going to try to make a difference in Lent. Please God, I'll try a little harder. The ashes are only external; it's what goes on behind the scenes, on the inside, that counts.

So, what do I do to make that difference this Lent? Well, that's up to you. Doing some small act of self-denial is always good: going off the chocolate biscuits, alcohol, or sweet things, for example. I gave up sugar in tea and coffee when I was a child. I couldn't go back on it now – I'd be poisoned, as it would be too sweet!

Fasting and abstinence is a time-honoured way of feeling some hunger and making a sacrifice. Traditionally, we are asked to abstain from meat on Fridays, especially during Lent. Meat was seen as a luxury once and perhaps not anymore, but it's still good to abstain and make that small sacrifice. Be sensible about giving things up and self-denial. And if you fall, get up and try again with God's help.

What about making a special effort to pay a visit to the church each day and going to daily Mass? When we visit the church, when we go to Mass, we tune into the Lord's presence. In prayer, we connect with the Divine. As one of our friars said, 'We get intimate with the ultimate.' And in prayer there are no calls dropped and it's 'always-on broadband'.

There is a lovely menu for Lent:

Fast from resentment. Feast on kindness.
Fast from lies. Feast on the truth.
Fast from cynicism. Feast on things that help.
Fast from negativity. Feast on being positive.
Fast from swearing. Feast on words that build up.

There are those who don't have to wait for Lent every year to go without. They have Lent with them all the time due to an illness or other struggles. I'd like to give a plug to the Trócaire box here. It's another way of making a difference in the lives of so many who have no choice but to struggle whether it's Lent or not. Lent is more what happens to us on the inside and how we reach out to others.

Blessings to you all for Lent. And remember, as Archbishop Fulton Sheen said, 'We diet for the sake of the body. We fast for the sake of the soul.'

'ST PATTY'S DAY'

There's no doubt about it: there's a lot of love for the Irish and the spirit of Ireland all around the world. If you look at social media and the mainstream media you will see pictures of many world-famous landmarks turned green for the day that's in it: the great statue of Christ the King in Rio De Janeiro, the Coliseum in Rome, and the Sydney Opera House to name a few. McDonald's are making green milkshakes these days, and green Guinness is served in many pubs to mark the occasion. The whole world is Irish on St Patrick's Day.

I ask myself the question: how much has the modern celebration of St Patrick's day actually got to do with his bringing the faith to Ireland? Today we see Patrick represented on parade floats in billowing green vestments, swinging a crozier around his head. Is there a danger that this will pass into the realm of fairy tale, along the lines of the departure of the snakes from the coasts of Ireland to drown in the sea? I notice today that people are more inclined to say 'Paddy's Day' or even 'St Patty's Day' and dress up in oversized green furry top hats and fake beards saying, 'Top o' the morning'. Here's a secret – we Irish never say that!

After dinner yesterday, I noticed someone had left in a box of shamrock for us. It is told that St Patrick used the petals of the shamrock to illustrate the relationship of God – Father, Son and Holy Spirit. It was a simple and ingenious way of explaining that there are three persons in the one God, like there are three leaves on the one stem, the mystery of the Holy Trinity. Today in Ireland, the fact that 17 March is the feast day of our national patron is not central to the minds of many people, I would argue.

Historically, the story of the bringing of the Christian faith to Ireland began before Patrick. Pope Celestine III appointed Palladius to go on a mission to the people of the Western Isles. Bishop Patrick came later, in the year 462, and had more success – in a sense the wind was at his back. He lit a flame of faith in our land which has been passed down from generation to generation. Over the centuries that flame was a fire and at other times it was just a flicker. During the Penal Laws, when the political system tried to extinguish the Catholic faith altogether, the flame still burned. When Daniel O'Connell secured Catholic emancipation in 1829 there was a resurgence of the Catholic faith in Ireland. Remember, Patrick just lit the candle, as it were; ordinary people have passed it on down through their families. As powerfully as Patrick handed on the Christian faith, and as generously as Irish missionaries travelled overseas with that faith, ordinary men and women passed it on too. Mothers and fathers, grandmothers and grandfathers brought their children to the church and told the children about Jesus Christ and it continues to this day. I see parents come to ask for their children to be baptised and I see grandparents bring them to the church to light a candle and say a prayer.

To quote Archbishop Fulton Sheen, speaking in 1974, 'I believe that we are now living at the end of Christendom. It is the end of Christendom, but not of Christianity. What is Christendom? Christendom is the political, economic, moral, social, legal life of a nation as inspired by the gospel ethic.' I believe this is happening in modern Ireland now and any attempts to ask why are being met by some with dismay, disagreement and even ridicule.

St Patrick brought the faith to Ireland. The Irish monks brought the faith all over Europe. For generations, Irish religious (nuns, brothers, and priests) travelled to developing countries to make a difference to the lives of the people there, armed not just with the gospels but with teaching, nursing, medicine, and other professional skills. But fundamentally this wouldn't have happened if it weren't for the generosity of mothers and fathers telling the stories of Jesus Christ to the children. The future of the faith in Ireland will be smaller perhaps, but people will choose to be part of it. The flame burns still.

GOOD FRIDAY

At first glance, the cross is *the* symbol of failure. Those who were crucified by the Romans were executed as 'non-persons' and they were crucified in public so as to dehumanise them even more. Crucifixion was designed to cause maximum pain and agony for the victim.

Jesus was crucified after a long night of being tortured, mocked, humiliated and brutally scourged with barbaric instruments made from bone fragments, metal and chain mail. He carried the instrument of his death, his cross, through crowds of people while being kicked and whipped along the way, and as he fell in exhaustion, he was pulled to his feet to continue.

When they came to the place of the skull, they crucified him along with two criminals on either side of him. As he hangs upon the cross, Jesus is made to look like a fool, one who called himself the King of the Jews. Pontius Pilate, Caesar's representative in that region who condemned Jesus to death, writes a death note. The note reads 'Jesus the Nazarene, the King of the Jews'. It is placed above Jesus' head as he hangs upon the cross. Although it is designed to mock him, in a strange way the Romans, who don't believe in God, proclaim Jesus a King by crowning him with thorns and placing a staff in his hand.

The cross of Christ is, to the onlooker, a symbol of shame, but looking deeper it is the ultimate triumph of a loving God who sent his only Son to be our Saviour. Jesus' death upon the cross is the theatre of redemption where we are all saved from our sinfulness. As we venerate the cross at 3.00 p.m. in all our churches we do so knowing that as Jesus says in John's Gospel: 'No one can have greater love than to lay down his life for his friends' (Jn 15:13).

> He was despised, the lowest of men, a man of sorrows, familiar with suffering, one from whom, as it were, we averted our gaze, despised, for whom we had no regard.
>
> Yet ours were the sufferings he was bearing, ours the sorrows he was carrying, while we thought of him as someone being punished and struck with affliction by God; whereas he was being wounded for our rebellions, crushed because of our guilt; the punishment reconciling us fell on him, and we have been healed by his bruises.
>
> We had all gone astray like sheep, each taking his own way, and Yahweh brought the acts of rebellion of all of us to bear on him.
>
> Ill-treated and afflicted, he never opened his mouth, like a lamb led to the slaughter-house, like a sheep dumb before its shearers he never opened his mouth ... (Isa 53:5–8).

WE ARE AN EASTER PEOPLE

The women of Jerusalem went to the tomb early on Sunday morning to anoint the badly damaged dead body of Jesus. They weren't able to do this after he was taken down from the cross, as it was almost the Sabbath and therefore Jesus was buried in haste. When they reached the tomb, they found that the huge stone had been rolled back. In the different gospel translations we meet different angelic figures who tell the women and the disciples that they won't find Jesus in the empty tomb.

From Luke's gospel we read:

> On the first day of the week, at the first sign of dawn, they went to the tomb with the spices they had prepared. They found that the stone had been rolled away from the tomb, but on entering they could not find the body of the Lord Jesus. As they stood there puzzled about this, two men in brilliant clothes suddenly appeared at their side. Terrified, the women bowed their heads to the ground. But the two said to them, 'Why look among the dead for someone who is alive? He is not here; he has risen. Remember what he told you when he was still in Galilee' (Lk 24:1–6).

Jesus is risen. He is no longer in the tomb, it is empty; the tomb cannot contain him anymore. Behind him, Jesus has left death, darkness, fear, and sin. As Christians, as people of the resurrection, we have no business in the empty tomb looking for Jesus – we won't find him there. We need to break free from the tomb too, and leave behind the darkness in our lives. We need to walk away from all that traps and binds us up in a suffocating grip. In the tomb we leave our fears, our phobias, our introspection, our prejudices, our anger, all violence, all rivalry, all darkness, and all sin. We run away from everything that takes our joy and stops us serving one another which is the key to contentment. We need to leave all this behind as all of it holds us back. We are called to go to Jesus who has gone ahead of us into the light, for he alone has the message of eternal life.

'Do not abandon yourselves to despair. We are the Easter people and hallelujah is our song' (Pope St John Paul II).

THE CAPUCHINS AND THE 1916 LEADERS

There will be much written about the Easter Rising in Dublin, the execution of the leaders, and the journey towards the signing of the Treaty of 1921 now that we are on the threshold of the centenary of 1916. We in the Capuchin order are already inundated with requests to see material contained in our provincial archives in Church Street. And various media groups, television, radio, and online, are contacting us for information.

The first the Capuchins heard of the Rising was a 'startling burst of fire' almost outside the door of St Mary of the Angels Church, on Church Street on that Easter Monday morning, 24 April 1916. They were just finishing their midday meal when all this began to happen. This was also following what would have been a busy time for the priests and the brothers in the friary with the Easter ceremonies. No doubt they were looking forward to some rest during these next few days.

Fr Columbus (Murphy) tells of rushing outside to meet walking wounded and a doctor ministering to a man shot in the arm. There were some accounts of soldiers of the Sixth Cavalry Regiment taking gunpowder to the Phoenix Park and coming under fire at the Four Courts. At this stage, no one seems to have any idea that the beginnings of a rebellion were taking place. Later, he learns of a small boy, John Francis Foster (2), being killed in his pram outside the Father Mathew Hall. The hall seems to have become a flash point as the week progresses as members of Cumann na mBan tend to people's injuries in the hall and the more seriously injured are taken to the Richmond Hospital.

Frs Columbus and Aloysius (Travers) are on duty that week supplying Mass in both Jervis Street Hospital and Gloucester Street Convent, so they are making their way over each morning through the chaos. Fr Columbus gives a very comprehensive account of the noise of incessant gunfire, the blast of cannon fire, and the eventual destruction of many buildings in Dublin city centre and especially O'Connell Street. He also risks serious injury and even his life to perform his priestly duties to those killed and injured.

As the week wears on and the casualties increase, the priests from Church Street continue to be involved in the relief work. This is perhaps because they are on the ground where the action is happening; also because they are hi-visibility in their religious habits. They endeavour to be honest brokers in ministering to those killed and injured and their families. Fr Columbus in his memoir tells of how on 29 April Padraig Pearse formally surrenders the GPO Garrison '[t]o avoid further slaughter', and Columbus travels with Elizabeth Farrell, a Cumann na mBan nurse, who attempts to convince Edward Daly at the Four Courts garrison that Pearse's surrender was genuine. This then spreads to the other garrisons over the next few days. Fr Aloysius (Travers) and Fr Augustine (Hayden) mediate negotiations between the British authorities and Thomas MacDonagh (Jacob's Biscuit Factory) and Éamonn Ceannt (South Dublin Union) for the peaceful capitulation of the men and women under their command.

When the leaders were imprisoned in Kilmainham Gaol and court-martialled, the Capuchin priests were called upon to come to minister to them and give them spiritual support. They were taken by car very late each night and driven to Kilmainham Gaol where they would meet the prisoners individually. By extension, they made themselves available to some of the families of the men too, and they also ministered to some of the women prisoners, most of whom were members of Cumann na mBan. Fr Columbus' memoir speaks of Countess Markievicz, who was in Kilmainham Gaol at the time of the executions and asked to receive instruction in the Catholic faith. She was later received into the church.

The executions began on 3 May 1916, when Fr Aloysius heard the last confessions of Padraig Pearse and Thomas MacDonagh. He was ordered from Kilmainham Gaol before they were executed. Later, following protests, the priests were allowed to remain present for the executions to complete the administration of the Last Rites of the Church. Tom Clarke was attended by Fr Columbus.

On 4 May, Fr Aloysius notes in his memoir that Fr Augustine Hayden ministered to Joseph Mary Plunkett; he also ministered to Michael O'Hanrahan, and William Pearse. Fr Columbus Murphy ministered to Edward Daly. Fr Albert Bibby, and Fr Sebastian O'Brien were also in attendance that night.

On 5 May, Fr Augustine was in attendance for John McBride.

On 8 May, Fr Augustine was in attendance at the executions of Éamonn Ceannt, Con Colbert, and Michael Mallin. Fr Albert Bibby was in attendance for Seán Heuston.

Finally, on 12 May, Fr Aloysius ministered to James Connolly (both before in Dublin Castle, and then in Kilmainham Gaol) and was in attendance at his execution. He notes that Fr Eugene McCarthy of James' Street and chaplain to Kilmainham ministered to Seán MacDiarmada earlier, but Aloysius then attended to him after the shooting.

Having read through some of the accounts of Frs Columbus and Aloysius (Aloysius much later ministered to Jim Larkin before his death in 1947), I can see the commitment, the bravery, and the selflessness of these priests who were primarily pastors of souls in their ministry. They were on hand night and day to try to bring pastoral care and hope to the many people who were deeply affected by the violence and chaos of the Rising. I have no doubt that they were also moved by the bravery of the 1916 leaders who were executed.

Humanly speaking, reading their accounts, I am also moved by how they stayed sane following what most have been a deeply stressful time for them seeing the things they did. Today those of us in ministry will be involved at times in critical incidents and we have structures in place to help us in our pastoral ministry.

In the days following the executions for example, Fr Columbus travels to Dundalk to give a two-week parish mission. He pens his memoir in the following months as a way of recording the week that was. I also believe he writes it to help him cope with what must have deeply ingrained itself in his soul – as it has done on the soul of Ireland, and indeed the world.

For Pope Francis, the church is at the service of Christ. The church is the vehicle for bringing about the kingdom of God here on earth through the power of the Holy Spirit. The church was established by Jesus Christ and he summoned twelve men, who he called apostles, to:

'Go, therefore, make disciples of all nations; baptise them in the name of the Father and of the Son and of the Holy Spirit, and teach them to observe all the commands I gave you. And look, I am with you always; yes, to the end of time' (Mt 28).

Like Jesus, who began his ministry over a small geographical area among the 'lost sheep of the house of Israel' to then crossing physical borders, the disciples moved across the world to bring the message of Jesus Christ to all peoples. Our people, our parents in the main, handed on the faith to us in their turn, and so we pass on the faith in Jesus Christ to those coming after us. It really is a labour of love.

It is no secret that the church in Ireland has suffered for the faith over the years, particularly in Penal times when there was persecution for Catholics and a price on the heads of priests and bishops. Yet through it all priests and people walked together and the old faith was passed on at the fireside and in the cradle.

I am the eldest of seven. My parents are grandparents and when we were young we went to Sunday Mass in suburban Dublin and at home we tried the family rosary with minimal success. My brother was an altar server – I never was. I grew up in the city so I never experienced the Station Masses or the Pattern Days. It wasn't till years later, when I was based in Rochestown, Cork, that I was invited to say a Station Mass. I can remember only one or two experiences of the May procession as a child.

For me the biggest religious occasion was without doubt the visit of Pope John Paul II to Ireland in 1979. I was almost ten years old and I guess the biggest impression left on me on the day wasn't the pope himself but the Aer Lingus 747 EI-ASJ call sign St Patrick. Being an anorak, I still love airplanes. I believe that my vocation to be a priest and a friar began way back in those days. Pope John Paul II made a big impression on me, even though the first thing I saw was that jumbo jet above the park. I've had a devotion to him ever since and, even though I never met him in person, I was lucky enough to be in St Peter's Square last year for his canonisation. For me, St John Paul's ministry is critical in that he taught us so many things but perhaps he reinforced the call of all people to sanctity – the universal call to holiness. This actually means that we are not merely called to be good Catholics or great Christians. We're called to be saints.

This is all down to my – our – call into a relationship with Jesus Christ by virtue of our baptism. As Isaiah says: 'And now, thus says Yahweh, he who created you, Jacob, who formed you,

Israel: Do not be afraid, for I have redeemed you; I have called you by your name, you are mine' (Isa 43:1). In an ideal world, we would all be daily conscious of our calling to ministry in the church and we would roll up our sleeves together and enthusiastically take part in our church where we are. But life is not like that and while there have been sincere efforts for collaboration in our parishes and pastoral areas, there are struggles and disillusionment.

In Dublin, Archbishop Martin has found it very difficult to make parish appointments this summer and priests are found working in parish groupings, which may entail big suburban areas with three churches that were three parish churches up to a few years ago. It can be demoralising for priests and people on the ground, when what we all want to be is missionaries where we are and what in fact can happen is maintenance.

But we can be missionaries. As priests in the parish grouping or in chaplaincy, in other words, where we are at the coalface in the service of the people of God – in collaboration with the people of God, we are called to be joyful missionaries. Pope Francis says: 'Priestly joy is a missionary joy. I would like especially to share with you and to stress this third feature: priestly joy is deeply bound up with God's holy and faithful people, for it is an eminently missionary joy. Our anointing is meant for anointing God's holy and faithful people: for baptising and confirming them, healing and sanctifying them, blessing, comforting and evangelising them.'

Pope Francis' connection with ordinary people is part of the way he is re-establishing a connection between the papacy and what he calls 'God's holy faithful people'. Priesthood is our privileged way of ministering to the people of God. I took that cue from a former General Minister of the Capuchin order, Canadian friar John Corriveau (who, incidentally, is now a diocesan bishop). He said that the Capuchin's life in community is our privileged way of witnessing the gospel.

Ministry is exercised in the name of Jesus Christ and his church and therefore the highest standards are to be kept. We minister to and with the people of God with whom we share a common vocation – baptism. We are at the service of what *Lumen Gentium* calls 'The People of God'. We are called to serve what the Holy Father calls 'God's Holy and Faithful people'. We need to equip ourselves with whatever we need to look after this high calling. We need each other.

You will remember, shortly after he was elected pope, Francis, in his homily during the Mass of Chrism in 2013, said this:

> A good priest can be recognised by the way his people are anointed: this is a clear proof. When our people are anointed with the oil of gladness, it is obvious: for example, when they leave Mass looking as if they have heard good news.
>
> This is precisely the reason for the dissatisfaction of some, who end up sad – sad priests – in some sense

> becoming collectors of antiques or novelties, instead of being shepherds living with 'the odour of the sheep'. This I ask you: be shepherds, with the 'odour of the sheep', make it real, as shepherds among your flock, fishers of men.

I love this image. I hope in my life I live up to this challenge. All over the gospels Jesus Christ crossed the threshold and into the house of the sinner. Jesus went to the margins to save the lost sheep. Jesus surprised people by calling Levi and Peter to be apostles. What kind of CVs would they have had, and if they met with a vocation's director would they get in? Jesus called all of us here because he needs us. He loves us.